The Rotisserie Cookbook

The Rotisserie Cookbook

**Over 75 recipes to revolutionize
your cooking**

Compiled by Lesley Mackley

COURAGE
B O O K S

AN IMPRINT OF RUNNING PRESS
PHILADELPHIA · LONDON

2003 Salamander Books Ltd
Published by Salamander Books Ltd.
8 Blenheim Court, Brewery Road
London N7 9NY, United Kingdom

© Salamander Books Ltd., 2003

A member of **Chrysalis** Books plc

This edition published in the United States by Courage Books, an imprint of
Running Press Book Publishers
125 South Twenty-second Street
Philadelphia, PA 19103-4399

1 3 5 7 9 8 6 4 2

Library of Congress Cataloguing-in-Publication Number 2002109165
ISBN 0-7624-1500-2

Notice: The information contained in this book is true and complete to the best of our knowledge. All
recommendations are made without any guarantee on the part of the author or publisher. The author and
publisher disclaim all liability in connection with the use of this information.

Credits

Project Manager: Anne McDowall
Commissioning Editor: Stella Caldwell
Designer: Cara Hamilton
Production: Ian Hughes
Colour reproduction: Anorax Imaging Ltd.
Printed in China

The recipes in this book have appeared in previous Salamander titles by other authors and have been
compiled by Lesley Mackley and edited by Anne McDowall for this edition.

Notes

All spoon measurements are level: 1 teaspoon = 5ml spoon; 1 tablespoon = 15ml spoon
Cooking times given are approximate: they will vary according to the starting temperature
of the food and its thickness.

This book may be ordered by mail from the publisher. But try your bookstore first!

Visit us on the web!
www.runningpress.com

Contents

Introduction

What we now tend to think of as roasting, that is cooking in an enclosed oven, is, strictly speaking, baking. Roasting originally meant cooking by exposure to radiant heat in the open, and long before domestic kitchens contained any kind of oven, meat was roasted on a rotating spit in front of a fire.

As the meat turned, the fat dripped into a container below, the outside caramelized to an appetizing golden brown and the meat juices within circulated to and fro producing tender, succulent, full-flavored meat. More recently, many butcher's shops and supermarkets installed rotisseries and their customers found that there is nothing more mouth-watering than the sight and aroma of gently turning, glistening and golden chickens, which somehow taste so much better than anything produced in an oven at home.

The main difference between the traditional method of roasting in the open in front of a fire and cooking in a modern rotisserie, is that the rotisserie is enclosed, creating a moister heat, which prevents the food from drying out.

Spit roasting at home

Some domestic cookers are supplied with a rotisserie attachment that can be fitted into the oven. These generally accommodate quite a large chicken or joint of meat and are very efficient. Some sophisticated grills incorporate a battery-operated spit, which rotates over, or in front of, the fire, and this is an excellent way of cooking when you wish to cook a large piece of meat for a party. Any of the recipes in this book for roasting on a spit are suitable for either of these methods of spit roasting.

The domestic rotisserie

If you do not have a rotisserie attachment for your cooker or grill, the good news is that domestic electric rotisseries are now widely available. There are several different brands of rotisserie on the market, and

The advantages of cooking in a rotisserie

- Easy to use
- Can be used anywhere
- Versatile - can cook a wide variety of food
- Fat drains off into the drip tray making it a healthy way of cooking
- The juice within the meat circulates around keeping it moist and full of flavor
- Built-in timer
- Easy to clean

although they vary in size, power, configuration, and price, the principle is the same. The domestic rotisserie is a self-contained unit that can be used anywhere there is access to an electric power point. It has a metal and plastic exterior and a metal interior with a clear viewing window in the door, through which you can see the food as it cooks. The heating element is at the back and the food rotates in front of it. The rotisserie also incorporates a temperature control and a timer.

There are two main styles of rotisserie. The most widely available has a horizontal metal skewer on which the food is placed for spit roasting. On the other type, the food is cooked vertically on an upright support. The disadvantage of the latter style is that it is not possible to cook stuffed poultry in this upright position.

In addition to the spit, the rotisserie also incorporates a flat adjustable basket, in which you can cook smaller items. Skewers are also included for cooking kabobs. Some models have a steaming tray, which enables you to cook vegetables or rice while the meat is roasting.

The Domestic Rotisserie

The Spit

The spit is used for roasting joints of meat and poultry. It is inserted through the center of the meat before it is positioned in the oven. The spit rotates in front of the heating element, allowing the meat to cook evenly. Larger models can accommodate two chickens or several smaller birds. Foods suitable for cooking on the spit include:

- Boned and rolled joints of beef, such as boneless rump roast
- Boned and rolled joints of lamb, such as leg and shoulder
- Boned and rolled joints of pork, such as shoulder, leg, loin
- Boneless turkey roasting joint
- Ham
- Chicken
- Small turkey
- Duck
- Game hen
- Pheasant
- Partridge

The Basket

The flat adjustable basket is used for cooking smaller pieces of food. They are held firmly in the basket, which is inserted into the rotisserie and rotates in front of the heating element.
Foods suitable for cooking in the basket include:

- Burgers
- Sausages
- Pork chops and steaks
- Ham steaks
- Lamb chops and steaks
- Steak
- Chicken breast fillets
- Fish steaks, such as salmon, tuna
- Quail

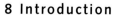

The Skewers

All rotisseries are equipped with a set of metal skewers for cooking kabobs. The food is threaded onto the individual skewers before they are positioned inside the rotisserie.

Foods suitable for cooking on the skewers include:

- Cubes of meat, e.g. lamb, pork and beef steaks
- Kidneys
- Rolls of bacon
- Cubes of chicken or turkey
- Firm fish, e.g. monkfish
- Prawns
- Scallops
- Vegetables, e.g. courgettes, peppers, aubergines, onions, mushrooms
- Tofu
- Fruit, e.g. pineapple, apples, figs, strawberries

Tips for using the rotisserie

- ◆ The instruction book provided with the machine will contain a chart of cooking times, but these are only a guide, so it is important to check that the food is thoroughly cooked before serving.
- ◆ The times given are for fresh or fully defrosted ingredients.
- ◆ The most accurate – and safe – method of ensuring the meat is thoroughly cooked is to insert a meat thermometer into the thickest part of the meat. (See the chart below for safe temperatures for meat and poultry).
- ◆ Meat and poultry should be well balanced on the skewer to enable the spit to turn evenly.
- ◆ It is not possible to insert the skewer into a joint of meat with the bone in, therefore joints should be boned and rolled up neatly.
- ◆ If you wish to stuff the meat, ask your butcher to leave it untied.
- ◆ Once the food has been placed in the rotisserie, allow it to rotate a few times to ensure that it will clear the element. If it is catching on the element, its position will need to be adjusted.
- ◆ To prevent food from sticking to the spit, basket or skewers, oil them before putting food on them.
- ◆ Use oven gloves when removing the food or handling hot racks.
- ◆ After removing a joint of meat from the rotisserie, allow it to stand 10 minutes. This will make the meat juicier and easier to carve.
- ◆ When cooking meat on the skewers, choose lean tender cuts that cook quickly.

Safe temperatures for meat and poultry

		Temperature on a meat thermometer
Beef and lamb	Rare	125°F
	Medium	140°F
	Well done	160°F
Pork		170°F
Poultry		175°F

Choosing, buying and storing meat and poultry

Today, many people buy meat from a supermarket, but if you have a chance to buy it from a traditional butcher, you will find that he can advise you on the best cuts for a particular purpose and will be able to tell you where the meat has come from and how long it has been hanging.

Meat should always smell fresh and the cut surface should appear moist but not wet. Check the fat too – it should be a whitish cream color and firm, rather than waxy, in texture.

If you have bought meat or poultry from a butcher, it will probably be wrapped in a plastic bag. Remove the bag when you get home and place the meat on a plate then cover loosely in aluminum foil, waxed paper, or plastic wrap. Place it in the coldest part of the refrigerator, making sure that neither the meat nor any juices from it can come into contact with other foodstuffs. Hot food should not be put into the refrigerator as it raises the temperature – cool cooked food first.

If you buy meat in an airtight tray from the supermarket it can be stored in the refrigerator, but place it on a plate to safeguard against leaking.

Meat from a supermarket will have a sell-buy date on it, otherwise follow these guidelines. Smaller cuts of meat, such as chops, have a relatively large surface exposed to the air and they will deteriorate faster than a large joint of meat. Offal, sausages, ground meat, and poultry portions should be used on the day of purchase. Pork, game, veal, and whole poultry should be used within two to four days, and beef, lamb, and venison, depending on the size of joint and whether it is being marinated, within one week.

Take a cool bag and ice pack when you go shopping for meat, so that it can be kept as cool as possible on the way home, and refrigerate all meat as soon as possible after getting it home. The refrigerator temperature should not rise above 41°F.

Before and after handling fresh meat, wash your hands thoroughly. Utensils and knives should be thoroughly washed after preparing meat, whether raw or cooked. Keep separate boards for the preparation of raw and cooked meat and poultry.

Marinating and stuffing

To add flavor to food before roasting, place it in a marinade for anything from half an hour to several hours or overnight. The oil in a marinade helps to keep it moist, and vinegar or citrus juice tenderizes meat. Herbs and spices give extra flavor. Meat, fish, poultry, and vegetables all benefit from spending a little time in a marinade. Allow the marinated food to come to room temperature before cooking.

Stuffings add flavor to meat and poultry and they can also help to keep the meat moist. Stuffing can be as simple as chopped herbs and garlic, or more elaborate combinations, which could include rice or couscous and fruit and nuts. Place the stuffing inside the cavity of a chicken and tie up firmly to prevent it falling out, or spread the stuffing over a boned joint of meat before rolling it up and tying firmly.

Sauces

Most roast meat, poultry, or fish will be enhanced if served with a sauce. Many of the recipes in this book include their own sauces, and the final chapter includes a selection of additional recipes for sauces, salsas, mayonnaise, and relishes that make excellent accompaniments to hot or cold roast meat or vegetables dishes. A small amount of juice from the roasting meat will fall into the drip tray and this can be added to a sauce or made into a simple gravy.

Chargrilled Tomato and Chilli Sauce (page 93)

Roasting on the Spit

Moroccan Roast Chicken

MAKES 4 OR 5 SERVINGS

2 TEASPOONS PAPRIKA

2 TABLESPOONS OLIVE OIL

3^1/2-POUND CHICKEN

2 TABLESPOONS BUTTER

1 ONION, CHOPPED

1 GARLIC CLOVE, CRUSHED

1^1/2 TEASPOONS GROUND CINNAMON

^{1}/2 TEASPOON GROUND CUMIN

3 TABLESPOONS BLANCHED ALMONDS,
FINELY CHOPPED

1^1/3 CUPS MIXED DRIED FRUIT,
SOAKED AND CHOPPED

SALT AND GROUND BLACK PEPPER

2 TEASPOONS CLEAR HONEY

2 TEASPOONS TOMATO PASTE

^{1}/4 CUP LEMON JUICE

^{2}/3 CUP CHICKEN STOCK

^{1}/2 TO 1 TEASPOON
HARISSA PASTE

◆ Mix together paprika and oil and brush over chicken. Put chicken in the rotisserie and cook at 425°F about 1^1/4 hours (20 to 25 minutes pound), basting occasionally, until chicken is cooked.

◆ Meanwhile, melt butter in a saucepan. Add onion and garlic and cook gently 5 minutes until soft.

◆ Add cinnamon and cumin and cook, stirring, for 2 minutes. Add almonds and dried fruit, season with salt and pepper, and cook 2 minutes.

◆ Transfer chicken to a carving board. Pour away any excess fat from the drip tray, then pour cooking juices into a pan. Stir in honey, tomato paste, lemon juice, stock, and harissa paste and add salt to taste. Bring to a boil and simmer 2 minutes.

◆ Carve chicken and serve with fruit mixture and sauce.

Caribbean Chicken

1 TABLESPOON CLEAR HONEY

JUICE 1 SMALL ORANGE

1/4 TEASPOON CAYENNE

1/4 TEASPOON FRESHLY GRATED NUTMEG

3 1/2-POUND CHICKEN

1/2 CUP CHICKEN STOCK

1/4 CUP RUM

SLICES ORANGE, TO GARNISH

◆ In a bowl, mix together honey, orange juice, cayenne, and nutmeg. Place chicken in the rotisserie and brush with honey mixture.

◆ Cook chicken at 425°F about 1 1/4 hours (20 to 25 minutes per pound), basting occasionally with honey mixture, until chicken is golden brown and cooked through.

◆ Transfer chicken to a heated serving dish and keep warm. Remove fat from the drip tray and pour cooking juices into a pan.

◆ Add stock and 1 tablespoon rum to juices in pan. Set over a high heat and cook, stirring, for a few minutes until slightly reduced.

◆ Just before serving, heat remaining rum, pour over chicken, and set alight with a taper. Garnish chicken with orange slices and serve with sauce.

Roast Chicken with Braised Root Vegetables

1/2 STICK BUTTER, SOFTENED

2 GARLIC CLOVES, CRUSHED

GRATED ZEST 1/2 LEMON

1 TABLESPOON CHOPPED FRESH HERBS, SUCH
AS TARRAGON OR PARSLEY

SALT AND GROUND BLACK PEPPER

3 1/2-POUND CHICKEN

OLIVE OIL

BRAISED ROOT VEGETABLES

8 SHALLOTS

2 MEDIUM CARROTS

2 MEDIUM PARSNIPS

1 LARGE POTATO

1/2 SMALL CELERIAC

1 SMALL RUTABAGA

2 TABLESPOONS OLIVE OIL

2 TABLESPOONS BUTTER

2/3 CUP VEGETABLE OR
CHICKEN STOCK

SPRIG FRESH THYME

SALT AND GROUND BLACK PEPPER

◆ Prepare vegetables. Peel shallots. Peel carrots and parsnips and cut into thick batons about 2 inches long. Peel potato, celeriac and rutabaga and cut into chunks.

◆ Place 1/2 stick butter, crushed garlic, lemon zest, chopped herbs, salt, and pepper in a bowl and beat together until thoroughly blended.

◆ Carefully ease your fingers between skin and flesh of chicken breast, taking care not to tear skin, and spread herb butter over flesh, easing a little of it down over top of thighs. Brush a little olive oil over chicken and season with salt and pepper.

◆ Place chicken in the rotisserie and cook at 425°F about 1 1/4 hours (20 to 25 minutes per pound), or until juices run clear when thickest part of chicken is pierced with a knife. Two thirds of the way through the cooking time, baste chicken with the juices that have collected in the drip tray.

◆ Meanwhile, cook vegetables. Heat oil and butter in a large heavy-bottomed pan. Add vegetables and cook over a high heat, stirring occasionally, until lightly browned. Add stock and thyme and season with salt and pepper.

◆ Cover pan and cook over a gentle heat 30 to 45 minutes until vegetables are tender.

◆ When chicken is cooked, remove it to a carving board, cover loosely with aluminum foil and let stand 5 to 10 minutes before carving. Serve carved chicken with braised vegetables.

Variation: The selection of vegetables can be varied according to availability and personal taste. Butternut squash, baby turnips or sweet potato make good alternatives.

Poussin with Watercress

1 CUP FRESH WHOLEMEAL BREADCRUMBS

3 TABLESPOONS READY-TO-EAT DRIED APRICOTS, CHOPPED

1 SMALL BUNCH WATERCRESS, CHOPPED

3 TABLESPOONS HAZELNUTS, CHOPPED

SALT AND GROUND BLACK PEPPER

1 SMALL EGG YOLK

1 POUSSIN, WEIGHING ABOUT 1³/4 POUNDS

WATERCRESS SPRIGS, TO GARNISH

WATERCRESS SAUCE

1 SMALL ONION, FINELY CHOPPED

1 SMALL BUNCH WATERCRESS, CHOPPED

¹/4 CUP DRY WHITE WINE

2 TEASPOONS CHOPPED FRESH TARRAGON

1 TEASPOON LEMON JUICE

2 TABLESPOONS PLAIN YOGURT

SALT AND GROUND BLACK PEPPER

◆ To make stuffing, mix together breadcrumbs, apricots, watercress, hazelnuts, and salt and pepper. Bind mixture together with egg yolk and use to stuff cavity of poussin.

◆ Place poussin in the rotisserie and cook 45 minutes at 425°, or until cooked through. To test, pierce thigh with a skewer: if juices run clear, poussin is cooked. Remove poussin from rotisserie and keep warm.

◆ To make watercress sauce, pour cooking juices into a pan. Add onion and cook gently, stirring occasionally, for 5 minutes, until soft.

◆ Add chopped watercress and stir well. Add white wine, tarragon, and lemon juice and heat gently. Stir in yogurt and season with salt and pepper. Heat gently to warm through.

◆ Pour sauce onto 2 warmed serving plates and place half a poussin on top of each. Garnish with watercress and serve.

Note: For a rotisserie without a horizontal spit, omit the stuffing.

Roast Stuffed Poussin

MAKES 2 SERVINGS

¹/2 OUNCE DRIED CHESTNUTS

3 TABLESPOONS RICE

1¹/2 TABLESPOONS SHELLED
PISTACHIO NUTS

1 TABLESPOON CURRANTS

SALT AND PEPPER

¹/2 TEASPOON GROUND CINNAMON

2 TABLESPOONS BUTTER

1 POUSSIN, WEIGHING ABOUT
1³/4 POUNDS

1 TABLESPOON BUTTER
FOR SPREADING

SALT AND PEPPER

◆ Put chestnuts in a bowl, cover with water, and soak several hours. Drain chestnuts, put in a saucepan, and cover with cold water. Bring to a boil. Cover and simmer 20 to 30 minutes, or until chestnuts are tender. Drain and let cool.

◆ Bring a pan of water to a boil. Add rice and cook 8 to 10 minutes until just tender. Drain and rinse with cold water.

◆ Chop chestnuts and pistachio nuts finely. Put in a bowl with rice, currants, salt, pepper, and cinnamon and mix well. In a skillet, melt butter. Add stuffing mixture and cook, stirring, until thoroughly combined. Allow to cool.

◆ Stuff poussin with chestnut and rice mixture. Spread a little butter over bird and season skin with salt and pepper.

◆ Place poussin in the rotisserie and cook at 425°F 45 minutes, basting occasionally, until thoroughly cooked and golden brown.

◆ Cut poussin in half. Serve with stuffing and cooking juices.

Note: For a rotisserie without a horizontal spit, omit the stuffing.

Peking Duck

MAKES 4 SERVINGS

1 MEDIUM OVEN-READY DUCK

1 TABLESPOON HONEY

3 TABLESPOONS DARK SOY SAUCE

1 TABLESPOON SESAME OIL

FEW DROPS EDIBLE RED FOOD COLORING (OPTIONAL)

TO SERVE

CHINESE PANCAKES (SEE NOTE)

6 GREEN ONIONS, CUT INTO LONG SHREDS

1/2 CUCUMBER, CUT INTO LONG SHREDS

HOISIN SAUCE, TO

Note: Chinese pancakes are available from Chinese supermarkets

◆ Place duck in a colander and pour over boiling water; repeat twice. Hang duck in a cold airy place or place on a rack in the refrigerator and leave overnight.

◆ In a small bowl, mix together honey, soy sauce, and sesame oil. Stir in food coloring, if desired. Brush duck evenly with honey mixture and let stand at least 1 hour.

◆ Place duck in the rotisserie and cook at 425°F, 20 minutes per pound, until juices run clear, basting occasionally with honey mixture.

◆ Remove duck from the rotisserie and let stand 10 minutes before carving.

◆ Serve carved duck on a warm plate with a stack of pancakes and with hoisin sauce, green onions and cucumber in separate bowls.

Duck with Pears

MAKES 4 SERVINGS

1 DUCK, CUT INTO 8 SERVING PIECES

2 SPANISH ONIONS, FINELY CHOPPED

1 CARROT, CHOPPED

2 BEEFSTEAK TOMATOES, PEELED, SEEDED, AND CHOPPED

1 CINNAMON STICK

1 TEASPOON CHOPPED FRESH THYME

1 CUP CHICKEN STOCK

1/4 CUP SPANISH BRANDY

4 FIRM PEARS, PEELED, CORED, AND HALVED

1 GARLIC CLOVE

10 ALMONDS, TOASTED

SALT AND GROUND BLACK PEPPER

FRESH HERBS, TO GARNISH (OPTIONAL)

◆ Place duck in the rotisserie and cook at 425°F, 20 minutes per pound, until juices run clear.

◆ Transfer duck to absorbent kitchen paper to drain. Transfer 2 tablespoons of oil from the drip tray to a deep skillet and heat gently.

◆ Add onions, carrot, tomatoes, cinnamon stick, and thyme to pan and cook about 5 minutes, stirring occasionally, until onions have softened but not browned. Add stock and simmer 20 minutes.

◆ Discard cinnamon stick and purée contents of pan in a food processor or blender or rub through a fine strainer. Return purée to pan, add brandy, and boil 1 or 2 minutes. Cut duck into 8 pieces then add to pan and heat through gently 5 to 10 minutes.

◆ Meanwhile, put pears in a saucepan into which they just fit. Barely cover pears with water and simmer gently until tender.

◆ Using a mortar and pestle, pound garlic and almonds to a paste. Mix in a little of the pear cooking liquid, then stir into sauce, if necessary adding more pear cooking liquid. Season to taste.

◆ Transfer duck to a warmed serving plate and pour over sauce. Arrange pears around duck. Garnish with fresh herbs, if desired.

Saucy Spit-roast Duckling

1 MEDIUM OVEN-READY DUCKLING

SALT AND PEPPER

2/3 CUP PINEAPPLE JUICE

SAUCE

1 POUND PITTED BLACK CHERRIES

1 GARLIC CLOVE, UNPEELED

2/3 CUP PORT

2 CUPS WELL-FLAVORED, STRONG BEEF STOCK

1 TABLESPOON FECULE OR POTATO FLOUR

2 TABLESPOONS BUTTER

1 TABLESPOON REDCURRANT JELLY

SALT AND PEPPER

◆ Prick duck skin in several places. Season inside and out with salt and pepper. Sprinkle inside with a little pineapple juice.

◆ To make sauce, put cherries, garlic, port, and stock in a saucepan and poach until cherries are tender. Remove cherries with a slotted spoon and set aside. Discard garlic.

◆ Blend fecule or potato flour with 2 tablespoons cold water, stir into liquid in pan, and bring to boil, stirring continuously until thickened. Mix in butter, redcurrant jelly, and salt and pepper to taste. Add cherries and cook until hot.

◆ Place duckling in the rotisserie and cook at 425°F, 20 minutes per pound, until juices run clear. Baste occasionally with pineapple juice.

◆ When duckling is cooked, pour away fat from drip tray. Mix roasting juices into sauce and reheat. Serve sauce with duck.

Quail with Grapes

MAKES 4 SERVINGS

*2-INCH PIECE FRESH GINGER,
PEELED AND FINELY CHOPPED*

8 QUAIL

1/2 STICK BUTTER, MELTED

SALT AND GROUND BLACK PEPPER

1 CUP SEEDLESS WHITE GRAPES, HALVED

1 CUP UNSWEETENED WHITE GRAPE JUICE

1 TEASPOON CORNSTARCH

FRESH FLAT-LEAF PARSLEY, TO GARNISH

*BULGAR WHEAT OR RICE, TO SERVE
(OPTIONAL)*

◆ Place some chopped ginger inside each quail. Brush quail with melted butter and season with salt and pepper.

◆ Place quail in the rotisserie and cook 20 minutes at 425°F, basting occasionally, until quail are browned and cooked through. Tilt birds to let juices run back into the drip tray. Transfer quail to a heated serving dish and keep warm.

◆ Pour away any fat from drip tray and transfer roasting juices to a pan. Add grapes and grape juice and place over the heat. Simmer a few minutes until grapes are warm.

◆ In a bowl, blend cornstarch with a little cold water and stir into sauce. Simmer until thickened. Season with salt and pepper.

◆ Arrange grapes round quail and pour sauce round. Serve with bulgar wheat or rice, if desired, and garnish with flat-leaf parsley.

Note: For a rotisserie without a horizontal spit, cook quail in the basket.

Spicy Roast Quail

MAKES 4 SERVINGS

1/2 SMALL ONION

1 GARLIC CLOVE

PINCH SALT

PINCH CAYENNE

1 TEASPOON GROUND CUMIN

1 TEASPOON GROUND CORIANDER

1 TABLESPOON CHOPPED FRESH CILANTRO

1/4 CUP OLIVE OIL

8 QUAIL

VINE LEAVES, PARSLEY AND LEMON SLICES, TO GARNISH

◆ Put onion, garlic, salt, cayenne, cumin, coriander, cilantro, and olive oil in a blender or food processor and process to make a paste.

◆ Place quail in a shallow dish and spread paste over. Cover and let marinate in a cool place 2 hours.

◆ Place quail in the rotisserie and cook at 425°F 20 minutes, until quail are cooked through.

◆ Serve quail on vine leaves, garnished with parsley and lemon slices.

Variation: Baby poussins can also be cooked this way.

Note: For a rotisserie without a horizontal spit, cook quail in the basket.

Pheasant with Golden Raisins

MAKES 2 OR 3 SERVINGS

1/3 CUP GOLDEN RAISINS

1/2 CUP MEDIUM SHERRY

1/4 CUP OLIVE OIL

1 YOUNG PHEASANT

SALT AND GROUND BLACK PEPPER

1/4 CUP PINE NUTS

◆ Put golden raisins in a small bowl, add sherry, and let soak.

◆ Rub 2 tablespoons of oil over pheasant and season with salt and pepper. Place pheasant in the rotisserie and cook 40 to 50 minutes at 425°F until cooked through and tender.

◆ Just before pheasant is ready, drain golden raisins, reserving sherry. Heat remaining oil in a skillet and cook pine nuts until golden. Add golden raisins and cook 1 minute.

◆ Carve pheasant and arrange on warmed serving plates. Scatter with pine nuts and golden raisins and keep warm.

◆ Pour cooking juices from the drip tray into a pan. Add reserved sherry and heat, stirring. Pour over pheasant and serve.

Tapenade Roast Beef

2 POUNDS BONELESS BEEF RUMP ROAST

1/3 CUP TAPENADE

1 TABLESPOON ALL-PURPOSE FLOUR

2 1/2 CUPS BEEF STOCK

2/3 CUP RED WINE

SALT AND GROUND BLACK PEPPER

◆ Untie beef. Make a deep cut along its length to form a pocket. Spread half the tapenade in the pocket. Fold meat back to enclose tapenade and tie up firmly with string.

◆ Place beef in the rotisserie and cook 1 hour at 400°F.

◆ Spread remaining tapenade over beef and cook an additional 10 minutes. Transfer beef to a warmed serving dish, cover with aluminum foil, and let stand in a warm place 10 minutes.

◆ Pour cooking juices from the drip tray into a pan and stir in flour. Cook, stirring, 1 minute. Whisk in stock and wine, bring to a boil, and simmer 10 minutes, or until reduced by half. Season with salt and pepper. Slice beef thickly and serve with sauce.

Mini Roasts

MAKES 4 TO 8 SERVINGS

2 1/2 POUNDS BONELESS BEEF RUMP ROAST

1 RED ONION, CHOPPED

1 SMALL GREEN BELL PEPPER

1 GREEN DESSERT APPLE

1 1/4 CUPS BEEF STOCK

2 TABLESPOONS OLIVE OIL

2 TABLESPOONS REDCURRANT JELLY

1 TABLESPOON TOMATO PASTE

1 TABLESPOON WORCESTERSHIRE SAUCE

1 TEASPOON ARROWROOT

1 TABLESPOON CRUSHED LEMON VERBENA LEAVES

◆ Cut beef joint through the grain into 4 cylindrical chunks. Discard string. Remove fat and cut it into 4 strips.

◆ Shape each piece of meat into a barrel by rolling with the hands. Place a strip of fat lengthwise down one side of each joint. Tie with string in 1 or 2 places. Place in a shallow non-metallic dish.

◆ Seed and chop bell pepper. Peel, core, and chop apple. Place onion, pepper, apple, stock, olive oil, redcurrant jelly, tomato paste, Worcestershire sauce, arrowroot, and lemon verbena leaves in a blender or food processor and blend until smooth.

◆ Transfer purée into a heavy-bottomed saucepan and heat, stirring occasionally, until boiling. Reduce heat and simmer, uncovered, 10 minutes until reduced by a quarter. Let cool, then pour over beef. Cover dish and marinade in the refrigerator 12 hours.

◆ Remove beef from marinade and place in the rotisserie. Cook 20 minutes at 400°F, basting occasionally with marinade.

Chinese Roast Beef

MAKES 8 SERVINGS

3^1/2 POUNDS BEEF ROUND

2 GARLIC CLOVES, THINLY SLICED

^{1}/2 TEASPOON CHINESE FIVE-SPICE POWDER

SEA SALT

^{1}/4 TEASPOON GROUND BLACK PEPPER

12 DRIED BLACK WINTER MUSHROOMS

8 POTATOES, QUARTERED

2 TABLESPOONS SUNFLOWER OIL

◆ With the point of a sharp knife, cut small incision in the beef and insert thin slices of garlic.

◆ In a bowl, mix together five-spice powder, 1 teaspoon salt, and pepper, then rub into beef. Place beef in the rotisserie and cook 1 hour at 400°F, basting at least once.

◆ Meanwhile, soak dried mushrooms in hot water 25 minutes, then drain.

◆ Cook potatoes in boiling, salted water 10 minutes. Drain well. When cool enough to handle, slice.

◆ Heat oil in a large skillet. Add potatoes and mushrooms and cook, stirring occasionally, 10 to 15 minutes, until browned. Serve with slices of roast beef.

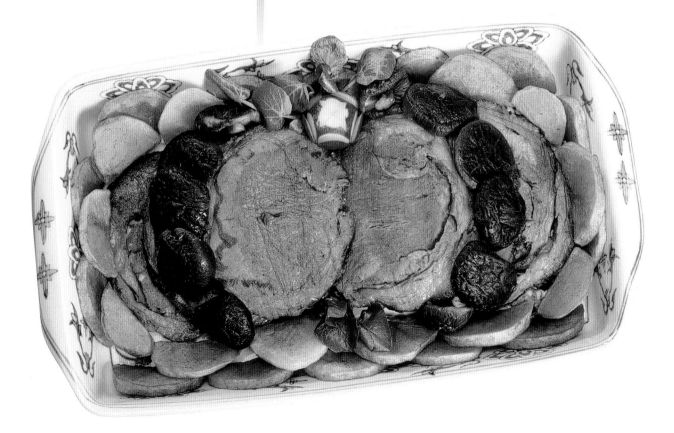

Spiced Pork Loin

MAKES 4 SERVINGS

1 TABLESPOON PAPRIKA

3 GARLIC CLOVES, FINELY CRUSHED

1 TEASPOON CHOPPED FRESH OREGANO

1/2 TEASPOON FINELY CRUSHED
CUMIN SEEDS

1 BAY LEAF, CRUSHED

SALT

3 TABLESPOONS OLIVE OIL

1 1/2 POUNDS BONED AND ROLLED
LOIN OF PORK

1/4 CUP FULL-BODIED DRY WHITE WINE

PITTED GREEN OLIVES, TO SERVE

◆ In a small bowl, mix together paprika, garlic, oregano, cumin seeds, bay leaf, and salt. Stir in olive oil.

◆ Place pork in a non-metallic dish and spoon marinade mixture over the top. Cover and leave in the refrigerator 2 to 3 days. Return pork to room temperature 30 minutes before cooking.

◆ Place pork in the rotisserie and cook 1 1/2 hours at 400°F.

◆ Transfer pork to a warmed serving dish. Remove fat from the drip tray and pour cooking juices into a pan. Stir in wine and boil 2 or 3 minutes.

◆ Slice pork thinly and serve with sauce. Sprinkle with green olives.

Stuffed Pork Shoulder

MAKES 6 TO 8 SERVINGS

*3 POUNDS SHOULDER OF PORK,
BONED AND SKINNED*

2 TABLESPOONS OLIVE OIL

2 TABLESPOONS BUTTER

2 LARGE POTATOES, CUT INTO CHUNKS

1 LARGE RUTABAGA, CUT INTO CHUNKS

3 PARSNIPS, CUT INTO CHUNKS

3 CUPS VEGETABLE OR CHICKEN STOCK

SALT AND GROUND BLACK PEPPER

1 TABLESPOON CORNSTARCH

1 TABLESPOON MANGO AND LIME CHUTNEY

SAGE LEAVES, TO GARNISH

STUFFING

*6-OUNCE CAN CORNED BEEF, FINELY
CHOPPED*

2 CUPS FRESH WHITE BREADCRUMBS

1 ONION, FINELY CHOPPED

1 TEASPOON DRIED SAGE

*1 TABLESPOON MANGO
AND LIME CHUTNEY*

◆ To make stuffing, mix together corned beef, breadcrumbs, onion, and sage. Add chutney and bind mixture together. Open out shoulder of pork and flatten. Spread stuffing along center of inside of pork.

◆ Roll pork into a round shape and tie securely with string. Season with salt and pepper. Place pork in the rotisserie and cook 1³/4 to 2 hours at 400°F, basting meat every 45 minutes.

◆ Meanwhile, cook vegetables. Heat oil and butter in a large heavy-bottomed pan. Add potatoes, rutabaga, and parsnips and cook over a high heat, stirring occasionally, until lightly browned.

◆ Add ²/3 cup stock and season with salt and pepper. Cover the pan and cook 30 to 45 minutes, until vegetables are tender.

◆ Transfer meat to a serving plate and keep warm. Remove fat from the drip tray and pour cooking juices into a pan. Stir in cornstarch, then gradually add remaining stock and bring to a boil, stirring. Add chutney and simmer 3 or 4 minutes.

◆ Slice pork, garnish with sage leaves, and serve with vegetables and sauce.

Florentine Roast Pork

MAKES 6 SERVINGS

2 1/4 POUNDS LOIN OF PORK, BONED

2 TABLESPOONS CHOPPED FRESH ROSEMARY LEAVES

2 GARLIC CLOVES, CHOPPED

SALT AND GROUND BLACK PEPPER

3 TABLESPOONS OLIVE OIL

2/3 CUP DRY WHITE WINE

CARROTS AND BROWN LENTILS, TO SERVE (OPTIONAL)

◆ Using a flat skewer, make deep incisions all over meat. Mix rosemary and garlic together with plenty of salt and pepper. Push rosemary mixture into incisions in meat. Rub any remaining mixture into flap where bones have been removed.

◆ Season pork well and tie up neatly with string. Rub meat all over with olive oil and place in the rotisserie. Cook 1 1/2 hours at 400°F, basting frequently.

◆ Transfer pork to a serving dish and keep warm. Remove fat from the drip tray and pour juices into a pan. Add wine and bring to a boil. Boil a few minutes to reduce slightly. Season to taste.

◆ Carve pork into thick slices, garnish with rosemary sprigs, and serve with sauce, accompanied by carrots and brown lentils if desired.

Roast Lamb with Garlic and Rosemary

MAKES 6 SERVINGS

3^1/2 POUNDS LEG OF LAMB

16 SMALL ROSEMARY SPRIGS

2 GARLIC CLOVES, CUT INTO 16 SLIVERS

1 TABLESPOON OLIVE OIL

2/3 CUP RED WINE

1 TABLESPOON ALL-PURPOSE FLOUR

2^1/2 CUPS LAMB STOCK

ROSEMARY SPRIGS AND GARLIC CLOVES, TO GARNISH (OPTIONAL)

◆ Use the point of a sharp knife to make 16 slits all over lamb and insert sprigs of rosemary and slivers of garlic.

◆ Place lamb in the rotisserie and brush over olive oil. Season with salt and pepper and cook at 400°F 1^3/4 hours, basting 2 or 3 times.

◆ Transfer lamb to a serving dish, cover and keep warm. Skim off fat from the drip tray and pour cooking juices into a pan.

◆ Add flour and cook 1 minute. Add wine and simmer 10 minutes, then add stock, bring to a boil and simmer 5 minutes. Season gravy to taste.

◆ Garnish with sprigs of rosemary and garlic cloves, if desired.

Roast Lamb and Vegetables

1 GARLIC CLOVE, CRUSHED

1 TEASPOON CHOPPED FRESH MINT

1 TEASPOON CHOPPED FRESH ROSEMARY

1 TEASPOON CHOPPED FRESH OREGANO

SALT AND GROUND BLACK PEPPER

1 SHOULDER OF LAMB, WEIGHING ABOUT 4 POUNDS, BONED

3 LARGE POTATOES, THINLY SLICED

1 LARGE ONION, THINLY SLICED

5 MEDIUM TOMATOES, SLICED

1/2 CUP DRY WHITE WINE

MINT, ROSEMARY AND OREGANO SPRIGS, TO GARNISH

◆ In a small bowl, mix together garlic, mint, rosemary, oregano, and salt and pepper. Spread herb mixture over inside of lamb, then roll up and tie into a neat shape with string.

◆ Place lamb in the rotisserie and cook 2³/₄ hours at 400°F.

◆ To cook vegetables, spoon fat from the drip tray into a large skillet and add potatoes, onion, and tomatoes. Pour over wine and season with salt and pepper. Cover and cook 1 hour, turning vegetables occasionally.

◆ Carve lamb and arrange on warmed serving plates with vegetables. Pour over cooking juices. Garnish with mint, rosemary, and oregano sprigs and serve.

Roast Stuffed Leg of Lamb

MAKES 6 TO 8 SERVINGS

4 POUNDS BONED LEG OF LAMB, PLUS BONES

SALT AND GROUND BLACK PEPPER

1 ONION, QUARTERED

3 TABLESPOONS OLIVE OIL

3 ROSEMARY SPRIGS

2/3 CUP DRY WHITE WINE

JUICE 2 LEMONS

STUFFING

1/3 CUP COUSCOUS

2 TABLESPOONS OLIVE OIL

1 SMALL ONION, FINELY CHOPPED

1 GARLIC CLOVE, CRUSHED

1 TEASPOON GROUND CINNAMON

1 TEASPOON GROUND CUMIN

2/3 CUP READY-TO-EAT DRIED APRICOTS, CHOPPED

1/2 CUP PINE NUTS

SALT AND GROUND BLACK PEPPER

◆ To make stuffing, place couscous in a bowl and cover with boiling water; let stand until absorbed and fluff up with a fork.

◆ Heat oil, add onion and garlic, and cook 10 minutes. Let cool. Stir into couscous with cinnamon, cumin, apricots, pine nuts, salt, and pepper.

◆ Place 5 pieces of string in parallel lines on the work surface. Place lamb, skin side down, across them and season with salt and pepper. Spoon stuffing onto meat. Roll up firmly and tie to make a neat shape.

◆ Place lamb in the rotisserie and cook 1¼ hours at 400°F, basting occasionally.

◆ Meanwhile, roast lamb bones and onion in a pan with 3 tablespoons oil 15 minutes. Add rosemary, wine, lemon juice, and salt and pepper and simmer 15 minutes.

◆ When lamb is cooked, remove from the rotisserie and let stand 15 minutes before carving. Remove fat from the drip tray and add cooking juices to the pan. Add 2½ cups water to the pan and boil until reduced. Serve gravy with lamb.

Cooking on the Skewers

Swordfish Kabobs with Puy Lentils

MAKES 4 SERVINGS

1/2 cup puy lentils, soaked

1 small red bell pepper

1 red onion

1/3 cup olive oil

1 garlic clove, crushed

Juice 1 lemon

2 tablespoons chopped fresh basil

1/2 cup pitted black olives, chopped

1 1/2 pounds swordfish steak, diced

◆ Drain lentils well, place in a pan, and cover with cold water. Bring to a boil, then reduce heat and simmer gently 35 to 40 minutes until tender. Drain.

◆ Seed and dice bell pepper and chop onion. Heat 2 tablespoons olive oil in a skillet and fry onion, bell pepper, and garlic 5 minutes. Add lemon juice, lentils, basil, and olives and simmer gently 3 minutes. Keep warm.

◆ Thread diced swordfish onto 8 skewers. Brush with a little remaining oil, and place in the rotisserie. Cook 10 to 15 minutes at 475°F, until golden and firm to touch.

◆ Stir remaining oil into lentil mixture and heat through. Spoon onto warmed plates and top with swordfish. Serve at once.

Louisiana Angels

MAKES 6 SERVINGS

9 slices bacon, rinds removed

18 button mushrooms

1 stick butter

2 tablespoons lemon juice

3 tablespoons chopped fresh parsley

Pinch cayenne

18 fresh oysters, shelled

Cornstarch for dusting

6 slices toast, crusts removed, cut into fingers (optional)

◆ Stretch bacon slices slightly with the back of a knife. Halve slices crosswise. Lightly fry bacon until opaque and still limp. Drain and set aside.

◆ Cook mushrooms in a pan of boiling water 1 minute. Drain.

◆ Melt butter in a pan. Remove from heat and stir in lemon juice, parsley, and cayenne. Keep warm.

◆ Dust oysters with cornstarch. Wrap bacon slices round oysters and thread onto 6 skewers, alternating with mushrooms. (Try to spear through the "eyes" of the oysters to keep them in position.)

◆ Brush skewers generously with flavored butter. Place in the rotisserie and cook 6 to 8 minutes at 475°F until oysters are just brown.

◆ Serve oysters and mushrooms on toast, or in the oyster shells if desired, with remaining flavored butter spooned on top.

Lime and Fish Skewers

MAKES 4 SERVINGS

12 ounces monkfish tails, skinned and cut into 3/4-inch cubes

12 ounces trout fillets, skinned and cut into 3/4-inch cubes

2 limes

1 teaspoon sesame oil

Large pinch five-spice powder

Ground black pepper

Strips lime peel, to garnish

◆ Place monkfish and trout in a shallow dish. Grate zest of one lime and juice. Mix lime zest and juice with sesame oil and five-spice powder. Pour over fish, cover, and chill 30 minutes.

◆ Halve and quarter remaining lime lengthwise and halve each quarter to make 8 wedges. Slice each piece of lime in half crosswise to make 16 small pieces.

◆ Thread monkfish, trout, and lime pieces onto skewers, brush with marinade, and season with pepper. Place in the rotisserie and cook 10 to 12 minutes at 475°F.

◆ Drain on absorbent kitchen paper, then place each kabob on a separate serving plate and garnish with lime peel to serve.

Garlicky Salmon Kabobs

MAKES 4 SERVINGS

2 TABLESPOONS LIGHT SOY SAUCE

1 TABLESPOON LIME JUICE

3 GARLIC CLOVES, FINELY CHOPPED

1 TABLESPOON SUNFLOWER OIL

1¼ POUNDS SALMON FILLET, SKINNED

16 TIGER SHRIMP, PEELED

SHREDDED LETTUCE, TO SERVE

◆ In a small dish mix soy sauce, lime juice, garlic, and oil.

◆ Cut salmon into 1-inch cubes. Place in marinade with shrimp and let stand in a cool place 1 hour.

◆ Thread salmon and shrimp onto 8 skewers. Place in the rotisserie and cook 12 to 15 minutes at 475°F.

◆ Serve kabobs on a bed of shredded lettuce.

Tuna Fish Satay

MAKES 6 SERVINGS

2 POUNDS FRESH TUNA STEAK

3 TABLESPOONS LIGHT SOY SAUCE

1 TABLESPOON SESAME OIL

1 TABLESPOON CLEAR HONEY

1 TABLESPOON DRY SHERRY

JUICE 1 LIME

1 GARLIC CLOVE, CRUSHED

1-INCH PIECE FRESH GINGER, GRATED

SATAY SAUCE

¼ CUP RAW PEANUTS, GROUND

JUICE 1 LIME

½ OUNCE CREAMED COCONUT

¼ TEASPOON CAYENNE

PINCH SUGAR

◆ Wash and dry tuna and cut into ½-inch cubes. Place in a large shallow dish.

◆ To make marinade, blend together soy sauce, sesame oil, honey, sherry, lime juice, garlic, grated ginger, and 2 tablespoons water. Pour over fish. Cover and let stand 1 to 2 hours, turning fish in marinade occasionally.

◆ Drain and reserve marinade and thread 6 cubes of tuna onto each skewer. Cover and keep cool.

◆ To make sauce, put ⅓ cup reserved marinade into a small pan and bring to boil. Stir in ground peanuts, lime juice, creamed coconut, cayenne, a pinch of sugar, and 2 tablespoons water.

◆ Simmer sauce over a low heat until coconut melts and sauce thickens slightly. Transfer to a small bowl and let cool.

◆ Place skewers in the rotisserie and cook 10 to 12 minutes at 475°F. Serve with satay sauce.

Mexican Fish Kabobs

1/4 CUP CHOPPED CILANTRO

1/4 CUP OLIVE OIL

JUICE 3 LIMES

4 TEASPOONS PAPRIKA

*1 FRESH RED CHILE, SEEDED AND
FINELY CHOPPED*

1 1/4 POUNDS RED SNAPPER FILLETS

4 MINI RED BELL PEPPERS, HALVED

2 ONIONS, EACH CUT INTO 8 WEDGES

GUACAMOLE

2 AVOCADOS

JUICE 1 LARGE LIME

1/2 ONION, FINELY CHOPPED

1/3 CUP TORN CILANTRO LEAVES

◆ To make marinade, place chopped cilantro, olive oil, lime juice, paprika, and chopped red chile in a shallow glass bowl and mix well.

◆ Cut fish fillets into chunks, add to marinade, and turn to coat evenly. Cover and refrigerate 2 hours.

◆ To make guacamole, mash avocados with lime juice. Stir in chopped onion and cilantro leaves and season with salt and pepper. Refrigerate until required.

◆ Remove fish from marinade and thread onto skewers, alternating with bell peppers and onion wedges.

◆ Place skewers in the rotisserie and cook 10 to 12 minutes at 475°F. Serve at once with guacamole.

Malaysian Shrimp Kabobs

MAKES 4 SERVINGS

1/2 CUP VEGETABLE OIL

1/3 CUP LIME JUICE

1/2-INCH PIECE FRESH GINGER, GRATED

2 LARGE GARLIC CLOVES, CRUSHED

*1 FRESH RED CHILE, SEEDED AND
FINELY CHOPPED*

*LEAVES FROM 1 SMALL BUNCH
CILANTRO, CHOPPED*

1 TABLESPOON LIGHT SOY SAUCE

1/2 TEASPOON LIGHT BROWN SUGAR

*1 1/2 POUNDS RAW, UNPEELED
LARGE SHRIMP*

DIPPING SAUCE

1 GARLIC CLOVE, CRUSHED

SMALL PINCH SALT

1/4 CUP LIGHT SOY SAUCE

2 1/2 TABLESPOONS LIME JUICE

*1 TABLESPOON VERY FINELY SLICED
GREEN ONION*

1 TEASPOON LIGHT BROWN SUGAR

1 OR 2 DROPS CHILI SAUCE

◆ In a bowl, whisk together oil, lime juice, ginger, garlic, and chile. Stir in cilantro, soy sauce, and sugar.

◆ Place shrimp in a shallow glass dish and pour over ginger mixture. Cover and refrigerate 1 to 2 hours. Return to room temperature 30 minutes before cooking.

◆ Meanwhile, make dipping sauce. Mash garlic with salt. In a small dish, stir together garlic, soy sauce, lime juice, green onion, and sugar. Add chili sauce to taste. Set aside.

◆ Thread shrimp onto skewers and place in the rotisserie. Cook 6 to 8 minutes at 475°F until pink.

◆ Stir dipping sauce and serve with hot shrimp kabobs.

Peppered Chicken Skewers

MAKES 4 SERVINGS

1 POUND SKINLESS CHICKEN FILLETS, DICED

1 TABLESPOON RICE WINE

1 TABLESPOON DARK SOY SAUCE

GRATED ZEST AND JUICE 1 LIME

2 TEASPOONS BROWN SUGAR

1 TEASPOON GROUND CINNAMON

1 TEASPOON SUNFLOWER OIL

1 TEASPOON SZECHUAN PEPPERCORNS, TOASTED AND CRUSHED

STRIPS LIME PEEL, TO GARNISH

LIME WEDGES AND SHREDDED CHINESE CABBAGE, TO SERVE (OPTIONAL)

◆ Place chicken in a shallow dish. Mix together rice wine, soy sauce, lime zest and juice, sugar, and cinnamon. Pour over chicken, cover, and chill 1 hour.

◆ Remove chicken pieces from marinade, reserving marinade, and thread chicken onto skewers.

◆ Brush skewers with marinade and sprinkle with crushed Szechuan peppercorns. Place in the rotisserie and cook 20 to 25 minutes at 475°F, until cooked through.

◆ Drain skewers on absorbent kitchen paper. Garnish with lime peel and serve with lime wedges and shredded Chinese cabbage, if desired.

Chicken Tikka Kabobs

MAKES 4 SERVINGS

2/3 CUP PLAIN YOGURT

1 TABLESPOON GRATED FRESH GINGER

2 GARLIC CLOVES, CRUSHED

1 TEASPOON CHILI POWDER

1 TEASPOON GROUND CUMIN

1 TEASPOON TURMERIC

1 TABLESPOON CORIANDER SEEDS

JUICE 1 LEMON

1/2 TEASPOON SALT

2 TABLESPOONS CHOPPED FRESH CILANTRO

12 OUNCES CHICKEN MEAT, DICED

CILANTRO SPRIGS AND LEMON WEDGES, TO GARNISH

COOKED PILAU RICE, TO SERVE (OPTIONAL)

RAITA

2/3 CUP PLAIN YOGURT

2 TEASPOONS MINT JELLY

1/2 SMALL CUCUMBER, FINELY CHOPPED

2 GREEN ONIONS, FINELY CHOPPED

◆ Place yogurt, ginger, garlic, chili powder, cumin, turmeric, coriander seeds, lemon juice, salt, and chopped fresh cilantro in a blender or food processor and blend until smooth.

◆ Place chicken in a shallow dish and spoon over tikka paste. Cover dish and refrigerate overnight.

◆ Thread chicken onto skewers and place in the rotisserie. Cook 20 to 25 minutes at 475°F.

◆ Meanwhile, make raita. Place yogurt, mint jelly, chopped cucumber, and green onions in a bowl and mix together.

◆ Serve kabobs on a bed of pilau rice, if desired, garnished with sprigs of cilantro and lemon wedges. Serve raita separately.

Cajun Turkey Kabobs

MAKES 4 SERVINGS

1 SMALL ONION, CHOPPED

2 GARLIC CLOVES, CHOPPED

1 TABLESPOON CHOPPED FRESH OREGANO

1 TABLESPOON CHOPPED FRESH THYME

1 1/2 TEASPOONS PAPRIKA

1/2 TEASPOON CAYENNE

JUICE 1/2 LEMON

1/3 CUP CORN OIL

1 1/2 POUNDS TURKEY FILLET, DICED

8 BABY CORN

8 SHALLOTS, UNPEELED

1 LARGE GREEN BELL PEPPER, CORED, SEEDED, AND CHOPPED

16 BAY LEAVES

◆ Place chopped onion and garlic, fresh thyme and oregano, paprika, cayenne, lemon juice, 1/4 cup corn oil, and seasoning in a food processor and blend to a smooth paste.

◆ Pour marinade into a glass bowl and add diced turkey, turning to coat well. Cover and refrigerate 4 hours.

◆ Blanch baby corn 1 minute. Blanch shallots 5 minutes, then peel.

◆ Thread marinated turkey onto skewers, alternating with baby corn, shallots, bell pepper, and bay leaves.

◆ Place kabobs in rotisserie and cook 20 to 25 minutes at 475°F.

Chicken Teriyaki

SERVES 8

1 1/2 POUNDS SKINLESS CHICKEN FILLETS, CUT INTO 1-INCH CUBES

3 x 8-OUNCE CANS WATER CHESTNUTS

1/4 CUP DRY SHERRY

1/4 CUP MEDIUM-DRY WHITE WINE

1/4 CUP SOY SAUCE

2 GARLIC CLOVES, CRUSHED

SUNFLOWER OIL FOR BRUSHING

◆ In a shallow dish mix together chicken and water chestnuts.

◆ In a small bowl, mix together sherry, wine, soy sauce, and garlic. Pour over chicken and water chestnuts, cover, and let marinate 30 to 60 minutes, stirring occasionally.

◆ Remove chicken and water chestnuts from marinade and thread alternately onto skewers.

◆ Brush kabobs with oil and place in the rotisserie. Cook 20 to 25 minutes at 475°F.

Thai-style Skewered Chicken

MAKES 4 SERVINGS

2 TABLESPOONS THAI RED CURRY PASTE

3 TABLESPOONS PEANUT OIL

2 TABLESPOONS GROUND CORIANDER

2 TEASPOONS GROUND CUMIN

*2 TEASPOONS SUPERFINE
GRANULATED SUGAR*

*2 STALKS LEMONGRASS,
VERY FINELY CHOPPED*

JUICE 2 LIMES

*4 SKINLESS CHICKEN FILLETS,
EACH WEIGHING ABOUT 5 OUNCES*

*LIME WEDGES AND COOKED RICE,
TO SERVE*

◆ In a large bowl mix together Thai red curry paste, peanut oil, ground coriander and cumin, sugar, lemongrass, and lime juice.

◆ Cut chicken into 1-inch cubes and add to marinade. Turn to coat evenly, cover, and refrigerate 2 to 3 hours or overnight.

◆ Thread marinated chicken onto skewers and place in the rotisserie.Cook 20 to 25 minutes at 475°F.

◆ Serve kabobs with lime wedges and cooked rice, if desired.

Malay Chicken

MAKES 4 SERVINGS

1 BUNCH GREEN ONIONS, WHITE PART ONLY, FINELY CHOPPED

2 TABLESPOONS CHOPPED FRESH CILANTRO

8 BONELESS CHICKEN THIGHS, WEIGHING ABOUT 1½ POUNDS IN TOTAL

2 OUNCES CREAMED COCONUT, CHOPPED

1 GARLIC CLOVE, CRUSHED AND FINELY CHOPPED

½ FRESH RED CHILE, CORED, SEEDED, AND CHOPPED

2 TEASPOONS SUNFLOWER OIL

1 TEASPOON SESAME OIL

2 TABLESPOONS LIME JUICE

2 TEASPOONS GROUND ROASTED CUMIN SEEDS

2 TEASPOONS GROUND ROASTED CORIANDER SEEDS

SALT

LIME SLICES

CILANTRO SPRIGS, TO GARNISH

◆ In a small bowl, mix together chopped green onion and cilantro. Open out chicken thighs and spoon an equal quantity of green onion and cilantro on each one. Reform thighs and place in a single layer in a non-reactive dish.

◆ Put coconut in a bowl and stir in just under 1 cup boiling water until dissolved. Stir in garlic, chile, sunflower and sesame oils, lime juice, cumin and coriander seeds, and salt.

◆ Pour coconut marinade over chicken, turn to coat, then cover dish and refrigerate overnight.

◆ Remove chicken from marinade and thread 1 or 2 chicken thighs onto each skewer with a lime slice.

◆ Place skewers in the rotisserie and cook about 30 minutes at 475°F, until chicken juices run clear when tested with the point of a sharp knife.

◆ Garnish with cilantro sprigs to serve.

Lamb and Apricot Skewers

MAKES 4 SERVINGS

3 TABLESPOONS APRICOT JAM

2 TABLESPOONS SOY SAUCE

1/4 CUP VEGETABLE OIL

2 TABLESPOONS CIDER VINEGAR

3/4 TEASPOON CAYENNE

2 LARGE GARLIC CLOVES, CRUSHED

GROUND BLACK PEPPER

1 1/4 POUNDS LAMB FILLET

4 SHALLOTS

4 FIRM, RIPE APRICOTS, HALVED

16 BAY LEAVES

◆ In a shallow glass dish, mix together apricot jam, soy sauce, vegetable oil, cider vinegar, cayenne, garlic, and black pepper.

◆ Cut lamb into 24 cubes and add to marinade. Toss to coat evenly, cover, and refrigerate 2 hours.

◆ Blanch shallots in boiling water 4 minutes, then remove and peel and halve them.

◆ Remove lamb from marinade and thread 3 chunks of meat, a shallot half, an apricot half, and 2 bay leaves onto each skewer.

◆ Place in the rotisserie and cook 20 to 25 minutes at 475°F.

Spicy Beef Kabobs

MAKES 4 SERVINGS

2 TABLESPOONS VEGETABLE OIL

1/4 CUP RED WINE

1/2 CUP BALSAMIC VINEGAR

3 TABLESPOONS GRATED FRESH GINGER

2 TEASPOONS PAPRIKA

2 TEASPOONS CAYENNE

SALT AND GROUND BLACK PEPPER

1 1/4 POUNDS BEEF ROUND

1 RED, 1 YELLOW AND 1 GREEN BELL PEPPER

16 CHERRY TOMATOES

◆ In a shallow glass dish, mix together vegetable oil, red wine, balsamic vinegar, ginger, paprika, cayenne, salt, and pepper.

◆ Cut beef into bite-size cubes and add to marinade. Toss to coat evenly. Cover and refrigerate 2 to 3 hours or overnight.

◆ Halve and remove cores and seeds from bell peppers and cut into 1-inch pieces.

◆ Remove beef from marinade and thread beef, peppers, and cherry tomatoes onto skewers.

◆ Place in the rotisserie and cook at 475°F 15 to 20 minutes.

Lamb and Bacon Brochettes with Red Onion

MAKES 4 SERVINGS

1 POUND LEAN LAMB

16 SLICES BACON

1/4 CUP CHOPPED FRESH SAGE

1/3 CUP OLIVE OIL

SEA SALT AND GROUND BLACK PEPPER

4 SMALL RED ONIONS,
UNPEELED AND HALVED

◆ Cut lamb into 1¹/₂-inch cubes. Remove rind from bacon slices and roll up each slice. Thread lamb cubes and 2 bacon rolls onto each skewer.

◆ In a small bowl, mix together sage and oil and season with salt and pepper. Brush all over prepared brochettes and halved onions.

◆ Thread onions onto skewers. Place into the rotisserie with lamb brochettes and cook 20 to 25 minutes at 475°F.

◆ Remove onions from skewers and serve with lamb brochettes.

Pork Kabobs

MAKES 8

JUICE $^1/_2$ ORANGE

2 TABLESPOONS OLIVE OIL

1 GARLIC CLOVE, CRUSHED

1 TEASPOON CHOPPED FRESH THYME

1 TEASPOON CORIANDER SEEDS, CRUSHED

SALT AND PEPPER

1 POUND LEAN PORK

1 ONION

1 GREEN BELL PEPPER

8 CHERRY TOMATOES

SHREDDED LETTUCE, ORANGE SLICES, AND
THYME SPRIGS, TO GARNISH (OPTIONAL)

◆ To make marinade, in a bowl, mix together orange juice, olive oil, garlic, thyme, coriander seeds, salt, and pepper.

◆ Cut pork into $^3/_4$-inch cubes and add to marinade. Mix thoroughly, cover, and refrigerate 2 hours.

◆ Cut onion into quarters and separate layers. Cut bell pepper into small squares, removing seeds.

◆ Thread pork, onion, pepper, and tomatoes onto 8 skewers. Place in the rotisserie and cook 20 to 25 minutes at 475°F.

◆ Serve on a bed of shredded lettuce, garnished with orange slices and thyme sprigs, if desired.

Kofta Kabobs

12 OUNCES GROUND LAMB

*4 SLICES WHITE BREAD,
CRUSTS REMOVED, CRUMBLED*

1 ONION, FINELY CHOPPED

4 GARLIC CLOVES, CRUSHED

1/4 CUP CHOPPED FRESH MINT

2 TABLESPOONS CHOPPED FRESH PARSLEY

1/4 CUP PINE NUTS, TOASTED

2 TABLESPOONS RAISINS

*2 TABLESPOONS CUMIN SEEDS,
LIGHTLY TOASTED*

1 TEASPOON GROUND CORIANDER

1 EGG, BEATEN

SALT AND GROUND BLACK PEPPER

OIL FOR BRUSHING

1 CUP SHREDDED ICEBERG LETTUCE

2 TOMATOES, CUT INTO WEDGES

1 ONION, SLICED

12 BLACK OLIVES

*WARM PITA BREAD AND LEMON WEDGES,
TO SERVE*

MINT DRESSING

2/3 CUP PLAIN YOGURT

1/4 CUP CHOPPED FRESH MINT

PINCH CAYENNE

SALT AND GROUND BLACK PEPPER

◆ Place lamb, crumbled bread, onion, garlic, mint, parsley, pine nuts, raisins, cumin seeds, ground coriander, beaten egg, and salt and pepper into a food processor and process briefly to combine.

◆ Divide mixture into 12 portions and shape each portion into an oval-shaped patty. Refrigerate 2 hours.

◆ To make mint dressing, mix together yogurt, mint, and cayenne in a small bowl and season to taste with salt and pepper. Refrigerate until required.

◆ Thread 3 koftas onto each skewer and brush with a little oil. Place in the rotisserie and cook 20 to 25 minutes at 475°F.

◆ Divide shredded lettuce, tomato wedges, onion slices and olives between 4 plates. Add kabobs and serve at once with mint dressing, pita and lemon wedges.

Variation: Ground beef could be used instead of lamb.

Lamb Kabobs with Salsa

2 GARLIC CLOVES, CRUSHED

1/4 CUP LEMON JUICE

2 TABLESPOONS OLIVE OIL

1 DRIED RED CHILE, CRUSHED

1 TEASPOON GROUND CUMIN

1 TEASPOON GROUND CORIANDER

1 1/4 POUNDS LEAN LAMB,
CUT INTO 1 1/2-INCH CUBES

SALT AND GROUND BLACK PEPPER

8 BAY LEAVES

PEEL 1/2 PRESERVED LEMON, CHOPPED

SAVORY RICE, TO SERVE (OPTIONAL)

TOMATO AND OLIVE SALSA

1 1/2 CUPS MIXED PITTED OLIVES, CHOPPED

1 SMALL RED ONION, FINELY CHOPPED

4 PLUM TOMATOES, PEELED AND CHOPPED

1 FRESH RED CHILE, CORED, SEEDED, AND
FINELY CHOPPED

2 TABLESPOONS OLIVE OIL

SALT AND GROUND BLACK PEPPER

◆ Mix garlic, lemon juice, olive oil, chile, cumin, and coriander in a large shallow dish. Add lamb and season with salt and pepper. Mix well, cover, and let marinate in the refrigerator 2 hours.

◆ To make salsa, put chopped olives, red onion, tomatoes, chile, olive oil, salt, and pepper in a bowl. Mix well, cover, and set aside.

◆ Remove lamb from marinade and thread onto 4 skewers, adding bay leaves and lemon peel at intervals.

◆ Place in the rotisserie and cook 20 to 25 minutes at 475°F.

◆ Serve kabobs with salsa, accompanied by savory rice, if desired.

Light Beef Satay

MAKES 4 SERVINGS

1 SHALLOT, FINELY CHOPPED

*1-INCH PIECE FRESH GINGER,
PEELED AND FINELY CHOPPED*

2 GARLIC CLOVES, FINELY CHOPPED

ZEST AND JUICE 1 LIME

2 TEASPOONS GARAM MASALA

SALT AND GROUND BLACK PEPPER

1 TEASPOON LIGHT SOY SAUCE

*1 POUND LEAN BEEF SIRLOIN STEAK,
CUT INTO 1/4-INCH STRIPS*

SATAY SAUCE

1/3 CUP UNSWEETENED SHREDDED COCONUT

2 TABLESPOONS CRUNCHY PEANUT BUTTER

1 TABLESPOON BROWN SUGAR

1 TEASPOON SUNFLOWER OIL

2 GARLIC CLOVES, FINELY CHOPPED

1 FRESH RED CHILE, SEEDED AND CHOPPED

1 TABLESPOON DARK SOY SAUCE

FRESH RED CHILE STRIPS, TO GARNISH

◆ In a small bowl, mix together shallot, ginger, garlic, lime zest and juice, garam masala, salt and pepper, and soy sauce. Place beef in a shallow dish and pour over marinade. Cover and chill 2 hours.

◆ To make satay sauce, place shredded coconut in a bowl and pour over 1 cup boiling water. Let stand 30 minutes.

◆ Place a fine strainer over a bowl and pour mixture through, pressing coconut with a spatula to extract all the water. Discard coconut. Blend coconut water with peanut butter and brown sugar.

◆ Heat oil in a pan and stir-fry garlic and chile 1 minute. Stir in peanut butter mixture and soy sauce and bring to a boil. Simmer 10 minutes, stirring occasionally, until thickened. Set aside.

◆ Thread beef strips along each skewer. Place in the rotisserie and cook 10 to 15 minutes at 475°F. Drain on absorbent kitchen paper.

◆ Reheat peanut sauce and serve with beef skewers. Garnish with red chile strips.

Vegetable Kabobs with Bell Pepper Salsa

1 LARGE ZUCCHINI, HALVED LENGTHWISE AND CUT INTO 1/2-INCH SLICES

16 SMALL FIRM TOMATOES

8 CHESTNUT MUSHROOMS

1 GREEN BELL PEPPER, SEEDED AND CUT INTO CHUNKS

1 YELLOW OR ORANGE BELL PEPPER, SEEDED AND CUT INTO CHUNKS

8 BABY ONIONS, OR 2 SMALL ONIONS, QUARTERED

3 TABLESPOONS OLIVE OIL

3 GARLIC CLOVES, CRUSHED

1 TABLESPOON LEMON JUICE

1/2 TEASPOON DRIED THYME

BELL PEPPER SALSA

2 RED BELL PEPPERS, SEEDED AND ROUGHLY CHOPPED

3 TABLESPOONS OLIVE OIL

3 GARLIC CLOVES

1 TABLESPOON RED WINE VINEGAR

8 SUN-DRIED TOMATOES IN OIL, DRAINED

1 SMALL RED ONION, ROUGHLY CHOPPED

2 TABLESPOONS CHOPPED PARSLEY

◆ Thread zucchini, tomatoes, mushrooms, chunks of green and yellow or orange bell pepper, and onions onto skewers. Place on a large serving plate or tray.

◆ In a small bowl, mix together olive oil, garlic, lemon juice, and thyme. Brush over vegetable kabobs.

◆ To make salsa, put red bell peppers in a blender or food processor with oil, garlic, vinegar, sun-dried tomatoes, and onion. Blend until very finely chopped. Season and add parsley.

◆ Place kabobs in the rotisserie and cook 20 to 25 minutes at 475°F.

◆ Serve hot vegetable kabobs with bell pepper salsa.

Tofu, Leek and Mushroom Satay

12 OUNCES PLAIN TOFU

3 LEEKS, TRIMMED

12 SHIITAKE OR BUTTON MUSHROOMS

1/4 CUP CRUNCHY PEANUT BUTTER

1 OUNCE CREAMED COCONUT

OLIVE OIL FOR BRUSHING

MARINADE

2 TABLESPOONS DARK SOY SAUCE

1 GARLIC CLOVE, CRUSHED

1/2 TEASPOON GRATED FRESH GINGER

1 SMALL RED CHILE, SEEDED AND CHOPPED

GRATED ZEST AND JUICE 1 LIME

3 TABLESPOONS SWEET SHERRY

2 TEASPOONS CLEAR HONEY

◆ Cut tofu into 12 cubes and leeks into 12 thick slices and place in a shallow dish. Wipe mushrooms and add them to the dish.

◆ To make marinade, mix together soy sauce, garlic, ginger, chile, lime zest and juice, sherry, honey, and 3 tablespoons water. Pour over tofu mixture and marinate several hours, stirring occasionally.

◆ To make satay sauce, place $2/3$ cup of the marinade into a small pan and add peanut butter and creamed coconut. Heat gently until melted, then stir until thickened.

◆ Thread the tofu, leeks, and mushrooms onto 8 skewers and brush with oil. Place in the rotisserie and cook 20 to 25 minutes at 475°F.

◆ Serve with satay sauce as a dip.

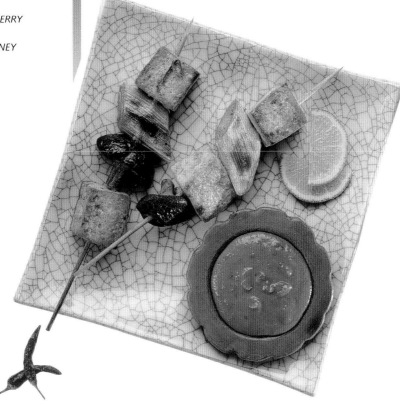

Patty Pan, Onion and Eggplant Kabobs

1/4 CUP CHOPPED FRESH CILANTRO

1/2 CUP OLIVE OIL

1 TEASPOON GARAM MASALA

1 TEASPOON DRIED CHILI FLAKES

2 GARLIC CLOVES, CRUSHED

SALT AND GROUND BLACK PEPPER

16 SMALL PATTYPAN SQUASH

8 BABY ONIONS, UNPEELED

8 BABY EGGPLANTS, HALVED LENGTHWISE

◆ To make marinade, mix together in a large bowl chopped cilantro, olive oil, garam masala, dried chili flakes, garlic, salt, and pepper.

◆ Boil pattypan squash 4 minutes, then drain. Boil onions 5 minutes, then drain, peel, and halve.

◆ Add pattypan squash, onions, and eggplant to marinade. Toss gently to coat evenly. Cover and refrigerate 2 hours.

◆ Thread marinated vegetables onto skewers. Place in the rotisserie and cook 20 to 25 minutes at 475°F.

Oriental Tofu Skewers

9 OUNCES TOFU

1 LARGE ORANGE BELL PEPPER

8 BROCCOLI FLORETS

8 CHERRY TOMATOES

SESAME MARINADE

3 TABLESPOONS VEGETABLE OIL

1 TABLESPOON SESAME OIL

1 TABLESPOON SOY SAUCE

1 TEASPOON GRATED FRESH GINGER

1 TEASPOON SESAME SEEDS

2 TABLESPOONS RICE WINE VINEGAR

1 GREEN ONION, FINELY CHOPPED

◆ To make marinade, mix together in a large bowl vegetable and sesame oils, soy sauce, ginger, sesame seeds, rice wine vinegar, and chopped green onion.

◆ Cut tofu into 16 cubes. Add to marinade, toss gently to coat, cover, and refrigerate 2 hours.

◆ Remove tofu from marinade, reserving remaining marinade for basting. Remove and discard stem and seeds from bell pepper and cut into squares. Thread tofu, pepper, broccoli, and tomatoes onto skewers.

◆ Place in the rotisserie and cook 20 to 25 minutes at 475°F.

◆ Just before serving, pour remaining marinade over tofu skewers.

Grand Marnier Kabobs

MAKES 6 TO 8 SERVINGS

3 FIRM APRICOTS

3 FIRM FRESH FIGS

*2 PINEAPPLE SLICES,
EACH 1 INCH THICK*

2 SATSUMAS

2 FIRM BANANAS

2 DESSERT APPLES

1 TABLESPOON LEMON JUICE

3/4 STICK UNSALTED BUTTER

3/4 CUP CONFECTIONERS' SUGAR

1 TABLESPOON GRAND MARNIER

1 TABLESPOON FRESH ORANGE JUICE

*1 TABLESPOON FINELY GRATED
ORANGE ZEST*

◆ Halve apricots and remove pits. Remove stalks from figs and quarter lengthwise. Remove and discard any woody core from pineapple slices, trim, and cut pineapple slices into chunks.

◆ Peel satsumas and quarter, but do not remove membranes. Peel bananas and cut into 1-inch-thick slices. Peel apples, cut into quarters, remove cores, and halve each apple piece crosswise. Sprinkle apples and bananas with lemon juice.

◆ Thread fruit onto 6 or 8 skewers, making sure that each has a mixture of fruit and starting and finishing with apple and pineapple.

◆ Melt butter, stir in confectioners' sugar, then add Grand Marnier, orange juice, and zest. Brush kabobs with sauce.

◆ Place in the rotisserie and cook 10 to 15 minutes at 475°F.

◆ Serve kabobs hot with remaining sauce.

Spiced Fruit Kabobs

MAKES 6 TO 8 SERVINGS

1 MANGO

1 SMALL PINEAPPLE

8 PLUMS

2 BANANAS

1 1/4 STICKS UNSALTED BUTTER

3 TABLESPOONS GRATED FRESH GINGER

1 TABLESPOON CONFECTIONERS' SUGAR

1 TABLESPOON LIME JUICE

◆ Peel mango, cut flesh away from pit, and cut into bite-size pieces. Peel and quarter pineapple and cut into bite-size pieces. Quarter plums and remove pits. Slice bananas. Thread a selection of pieces of fruit onto each skewer.

◆ Melt butter and stir in fresh ginger, confectioners' sugar, and lime juice. Brush over kabobs.

◆ Place kabobs in rotisserie and cook 10 to 15 minutes at 475°F.

Caramel Fruit Kabobs with Mousseline Sauce

MAKES 4 TO 6 SERVINGS

1 TABLESPOON LEMON JUICE

3 TABLESPOONS BRANDY

1 OR 2 TABLESPOONS CLEAR HONEY

1/2 CUP ORANGE JUICE

CINNAMON STICK, BROKEN INTO PIECES

1 SMALL PINEAPPLE

3 PEACHES

2 BANANAS

BUNCH SEEDLESS GRAPES

18 LARGE STRAWBERRIES

1/2 STICK BUTTER, MELTED

2 TABLESPOONS SUPERFINE GRANULATED SUGAR

MOUSSELINE SAUCE

1 EGG, PLUS 1 EXTRA YOLK

3 TABLESPOONS SUPERFINE GRANULATED SUGAR

2 TABLESPOONS CREAM SHERRY

◆ In a large bowl mix together lemon juice, brandy, honey, orange juice, and broken cinnamon stick.

◆ To prepare fruit, cut pineapple into thick slices, then peel, discard core, and cut flesh into chunks. Skin peaches and cut flesh into chunks. Cut bananas into 1-inch pieces.

◆ Add pineapple, peaches, bananas, and grapes to marinade and stir gently to coat evenly. Let stand 2 hours. Add whole strawberries to marinade 15 minutes before end of marinating time.

◆ Drain fruit and thread fruit onto 4 to 6 kabobs. Brush with melted butter and sprinkle with sugar. Place in the rotisserie and cook 10 to 15 minutes at 475°F.

◆ Meanwhile, make mousseline sauce. Place egg and extra yolk, sugar, and sherry into the top of a double boiler or a bowl set over a saucepan of simmering water. Using a balloon whisk, whisk together until very thick and foamy. This will take at least 10 minutes.

◆ Serve sauce with fruit kabobs.

Cooking in the Basket

Marinated Tuna Steaks

MAKES 4 SERVINGS

1 SMALL ONION, FINELY CHOPPED

4 GREEN ONIONS, FINELY CHOPPED

2 GARLIC CLOVES, CRUSHED

1-INCH PIECE FRESH GINGER, GRATED

1/2 TEASPOON HOT PEPPER SAUCE

SALT

4 TUNA STEAKS, EACH 3/4 INCH THICK

CUCUMBER SALAD

1 CUCUMBER, PEELED, SEEDED
AND CHOPPED

1 TEASPOON SALT

1 GARLIC CLOVE, CRUSHED

1 TABLESPOON LIME JUICE

1 SMALL FRESH RED CHILE,
SEEDED AND FINELY CHOPPED

◆ To make marinade, in a shallow dish, mix together onion, green onions, garlic, ginger, hot pepper sauce, and salt to taste.

◆ Place tuna steaks in dish and spoon marinade over to coat. Cover and refrigerate 2 hours.

◆ To make cucumber salad, mix cucumber and salt together and place in a colander. Let stand 10 minutes. Pat dry with absorbent kitchen paper. In a bowl, mix together cucumber, garlic, lime juice, and chile.

◆ Put tuna in the basket and place in the rotisserie. Cook at 425°F 20 to 25 minutes. Serve with cucumber salad.

Salmon with Avocado Salsa

MAKES 4 SERVINGS

*4 SALMON FILLETS WITH SKIN,
EACH WEIGHING ABOUT 6 OUNCES*

OLIVE OIL

SEA SALT AND PEPPER

*LIME WEDGES AND CILANTRO
LEAVES, TO GARNISH*

SALSA

1 RIPE BUT FIRM AVOCADO

*2 LARGE RIPE TOMATOES, PEELED,
SEEDED, AND FINELY CHOPPED*

1/2 SMALL RED ONION, FINELY CHOPPED

*1/2 OR 1 FRESH RED CHILE,
SEEDED AND THINLY SLICED*

1 GARLIC CLOVE, FINELY CHOPPED

2 TABLESPOONS LIME JUICE

*2 TABLESPOONS CHOPPED
FRESH CILANTRO*

SALT AND PEPPER

◆ To make salsa, halve avocado, discard pit, quarter each half, and remove skin. Dice avocado flesh.

◆ In a bowl, mix together avocado, tomatoes, red onion, chile, garlic, lime juice, cilantro, and salt and pepper. Cover and refrigerate 1 hour.

◆ Dry fish well, then brush skin with some olive oil.

◆ Put salmon in the basket and place in the rotisserie. Cook 15 to 20 minutes at 425°F.

◆ Season salmon with sea salt and pepper, garnish with lime wedges and cilantro leaves, and serve with salsa.

Chinese-style Salmon Steaks

MAKES 4 SERVINGS

2 TABLESPOONS HOISIN SAUCE

2 TABLESPOONS DARK SOY SAUCE

1 TEASPOON SESAME OIL

1/4 TEASPOON FIVE-SPICE POWDER

2 TEASPOONS CLEAR HONEY

1 GARLIC CLOVE, CRUSHED

1 TEASPOON GRATED FRESH GINGER

4 SALMON STEAKS, EACH WEIGHING ABOUT
5 OUNCES, WASHED AND DRIED

◆ In a bowl mix together hoisin sauce, soy sauce, sesame oil, five-spice powder, honey, garlic, and ginger.

◆ Brush each salmon steak with the glaze and put in the basket. Place in the rotisserie and cook 20 to 25 minutes at 425°F.

◆ Serve at once, with a green salad and garlic bread if desired.

Mackerel with Rhubarb Sauce

MAKES 4 SERVINGS

4 FRESH MACKEREL

SALT AND PEPPER

SALAD OIL FOR BRUSHING

RHUBARB SAUCE

2 OR 3 STALKS RHUBARB, TRIMMED

1 TEASPOON LEMON JUICE

3 TABLESPOONS SWEET CIDER

2 TABLESPOONS DEMERARA SUGAR

1/4 TEASPOON GRATED NUTMEG

◆ Clean and gut mackerel, remove and discard heads. Season insides with salt and pepper to taste. Brush all over with oil.

◆ To make sauce, place rhubarb, lemon juice, cider, sugar, and nutmeg in a heavy-bottomed saucepan. Cover and cook gently, shaking pan occasionally until rhubarb is very soft.

◆ Transfer rhubarb to a blender and purée. Return to pan, cover, and keep hot.

◆ Put mackerel in the basket and place in the rotisserie. Cook 20 to 30 minutes at 425°F.

◆ Serve grilled mackerel with hot rhubarb sauce.

Sardines in Vine Leaves

MAKES 4 TO 6 SERVINGS

*3 UNWAXED THIN-SKINNED LEMONS,
QUARTERED LENGTHWISE*

3 TABLESPOONS SEA SALT

2 TABLESPOONS SUGAR

12 LARGE VINE LEAVES IN BRINE

12 FRESH SARDINES, SCALED AND GUTTED

SALAD LEAVES, TO GARNISH

STUFFING

1/4 CUP CHOPPED FRESH CILANTRO

1/4 CUP CHOPPED FRESH PARSLEY

2 GARLIC CLOVES, CRUSHED

SALT AND GROUND BLACK PEPPER

1/4 CUP OLIVE OIL

◆ Preheat oven to 375°F. Place lemon quarters in an ovenproof dish with salt and sugar and mix well. Cover with aluminum foil and bake 1 to 1¹/2 hours until soft. Let cool.

◆ Place vine leaves in a bowl and cover with cold water. Let soak 1 hour, changing water twice. Drain and pat dry.

◆ Remove backbone from sardines by pressing down along length of backbone to flatten. Pull out backbone and wash and dry fish.

◆ To make stuffing, in a bowl mix together cilantro, parsley, garlic, salt, pepper, and olive oil. Stuff fish with herb mixture.

◆ Roll up each fish in a vine leaf. Put in the basket and place in the rotisserie. Cook 20 to 25 minutes at 425°F until vine leaves are crisp and fish flakes easily when tested with the point of a knife.

◆ Garnish fish with salad leaves and serve with roasted lemons.

Lobster with Herb Butter

MAKES 2 SERVINGS

*2 RAW LOBSTERS, EACH WEIGHING ABOUT
1 POUND, SPLIT IN HALF LENGTHWISE WITH
CLAWS CRACKED*

SALT AND GROUND BLACK PEPPER

HERB BUTTER

3 TABLESPOONS BUTTER, SOFTENED

1 TABLESPOON CHOPPED FRESH CHERVIL

1 TEASPOON SNIPPED FRESH CHIVES

1 TEASPOON FINELY CHOPPED SHALLOT

SQUEEZE LEMON JUICE

◆ To make herb butter, put butter, chervil, chives, shallot, lemon juice, and salt and pepper into a bowl and beat together to combine.

◆ Place flavored butter in a sausage shape on a piece of waxed paper or plastic wrap. Roll up to produce a cylinder and refrigerate to harden.

◆ Season lobster flesh lightly with salt and pepper. Put in the basket and place in the rotisserie. Cook 20 to 30 minutes at 425°F, until flesh has become opaque and shells have turned orange.

◆ Serve freshly cooked lobster with discs of herb butter.

Chicken with Lemongrass

MAKES 4 TO 6 SERVINGS

3-POUND CHICKEN, CUT INTO 8 PIECES

4 THICK STALKS LEMONGRASS

4 GREEN ONIONS, CHOPPED

4 BLACK PEPPERCORNS, CRACKED

2 TABLESPOONS VEGETABLE OIL

FRESH RED CHILE, CUT INTO THIN SLIVERS, TO GARNISH

◆ With the point of a sharp knife, cut slashes in each chicken piece. Place in a shallow dish.

◆ Chop lower parts of lemongrass stalks, then pound with green onions and peppercorns using a mortar and pestle. Spread over chicken and into slashes. Cover and set aside 2 hours.

◆ Put chicken pieces in the basket and place in the rotisserie. Cook 25 to 30 minutes at 425°F.

◆ Transfer chicken pieces to a warmed serving dish, spoon over cooking juices that have collected in the drip tray, and sprinkle with red chill to serve.

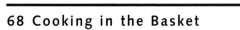

Tandoori Chicken

MAKES 4 SERVINGS

2^1/2 POUNDS CHICKEN JOINTS, SKINNED

3 TEASPOONS LIME JUICE

SALT

1 TEASPOON CORIANDER SEEDS

1 TEASPOON CUMIN SEEDS

1 TEASPOON CAYENNE

2 TEASPOONS GARAM MASALA

1-INCH PIECE FRESH GINGER, GRATED

1 SMALL ONION, ROUGHLY CHOPPED

1^1/4 CUPS PLAIN YOGURT

LIME WEDGES AND CILANTRO SPRIGS, TO GARNISH

◆ Wash chicken joints and pat dry with absorbent kitchen paper. Slash meaty parts 2 or 3 times. Place chicken in a shallow non-metallic dish. Sprinkle with lime juice and salt and set aside.

◆ Using a mortar and pestle, crush coriander and cumin seeds. Put into a blender or food processor fitted with a metal blade. Add cayenne, garam masala, ginger, onion, and yogurt and process until smooth and frothy.

◆ Pour marinade over chicken and cover loosely. Refrigerate 6 hours or overnight.

◆ Drain excess marinade from chicken joints. Put chicken in the basket and place in the rotisserie. Cook 25 to 30 minutes at 425°F.

◆ Serve chicken hot, garnished with lime wedges and sprigs of cilantro.

Chinese Chicken

4 CHICKEN QUARTERS, EACH WEIGHING
ABOUT 8 OUNCES

2 GARLIC CLOVES, FINELY CHOPPED

1-INCH PIECE FRESH GINGER,
PEELED AND FINELY CHOPPED

1/4 CUP HOISIN SAUCE

2 TABLESPOONS DRY SHERRY

1 TEASPOON CHILI SAUCE

1 TABLESPOON DARK SOY SAUCE

1 TABLESPOON BROWN SUGAR

1 TABLESPOON SNIPPED FRESH CHIVES,
TO GARNISH

◆ Remove skin and fat from chicken quarters. Rinse and pat dry with absorbent kitchen paper. Using a sharp knife, score top of chicken pieces in diagonal lines. Place chicken in a shallow dish.

◆ In a bowl, mix together garlic, ginger, hoisin sauce, sherry, chili sauce, soy sauce, and sugar. Spoon over prepared chicken pieces. Cover and refrigerate overnight.

◆ Put chicken in the basket and place in the rotisserie. Cook 30 to 35 minutes at 425°F. Garnish with snipped chives to serve.

Chicken with Rosemary

4 CHICKEN BREASTS, ON THE BONE,
EACH WEIGHING ABOUT 6 OUNCES

2 GARLIC CLOVES, PEELED AND SLICED

4 FRESH ROSEMARY SPRIGS

1/3 CUP OLIVE OIL

GRATED ZEST AND JUICE 1/2 LEMON

2 TABLESPOONS DRY WHITE WINE

SALT AND PEPPER

1/2 TEASPOON DIJON-STYLE MUSTARD

2 TABLESPOONS BALSAMIC VINEGAR

1 TEASPOON SUGAR

◆ Make several incisions in chicken breasts and insert pieces of garlic and rosemary. Place chicken breasts in a flameproof dish.

◆ In a small bowl, mix together 2 tablespoons olive oil with lemon zest and juice, white wine, and salt and pepper. Pour over chicken breasts and let marinate 45 minutes.

◆ Put chicken breasts in the basket and place in the rotisserie. Cook 20 to 25 minutes at 425°F.

◆ In a bowl, whisk together mustard, vinegar, sugar, salt and pepper, and remaining oil. Add any cooking juices or marinade from pan and spoon over chicken to serve.

Californian Chicken and Avocado Salad

MAKES 4 SERVINGS

1/3 CUP OLIVE OIL

1 TEASPOON DRIED OREGANO

SALT AND PEPPER

4 LARGE CHICKEN FILLETS

2 GARLIC CLOVES

1 TABLESPOON RED WINE VINEGAR

GRATED ZEST AND JUICE 1 SMALL ORANGE

2 LARGE AVOCADOS

3 TOMATOES, DICED

1 TABLESPOON CHOPPED MINT LEAVES OR PARSLEY

MIXED SALAD LEAVES, TO SERVE

1 SMALL RED ONION, CUT INTO RINGS, TO GARNISH

◆ In a small bowl mix together 1 tablespoon olive oil and dried oregano and season with salt and pepper. Rub over skinless side of chicken fillets.

◆ Put chicken fillets in the basket and place in the rotisserie. Cook 25 to 30 minutes at 425°F until cooked through. Cool.

◆ Meanwhile, crush garlic and mix to a paste with a little oil. Whisk in red wine vinegar, remaining oil, orange zest, and 3 tablespoons orange juice. Season with salt and pepper.

◆ Remove and discard chicken skin. Cut chicken into thin strips and place in a large bowl. Pour over dressing.

◆ Halve avocados and discard pit. Use a small melon-ball cutter to scroop the flesh into balls. Mix into chicken with tomatoes and mint. Toss gently.

◆ Arrange lettuce leaves on plates. Top with salad and garnish with onions rings.

Chicken with Cilantro

MAKES 2 TO 4 SERVINGS

6 CILANTRO SPRIGS

1 TABLESPOON BLACK PEPPERCORNS, CRUSHED

2 GARLIC CLOVES, CHOPPED

JUICE 1 LIME

2 TEASPOONS FISH SAUCE

4 LARGE CHICKEN DRUMSTICKS OR THIGHS

LIME WEDGES, TO SERVE

◆ Using a mortar and pestle or small blender, pound or mix together cilantro, peppercorns, garlic, lime juice, and fish sauce. Set aside.

◆ Using the point of a sharp knife, cut slashes in chicken. Spread spice mixture over chicken. Cover and refrigerate 2 to 3 hours, turning occasionally.

◆ Put chicken pieces in the basket and place in the rotisserie. Cook 25 to 30 minutes at 425°F until cooked through and golden. Serve with wedges of lime.

Hummus and Chicken Toasts

MAKES 4 TO 8 SERVINGS

2 SKINLESS CHICKEN FILLETS

JUICE 1/2 LEMON

1/3 CUP OLIVE OIL

SALT AND GROUND BLACK PEPPER

2 TEASPOONS SESAME SEEDS, TOASTED

1 TEASPOON GROUND CUMIN

1/2 TEASPOON PAPRIKA

8 SLICES CIABATTA-TYPE BREAD

SALAD LEAVES, TO GARNISH

HUMMUS

15-OUNCE CAN CHICKPEAS, DRAINED

1/4 CUP TAHINI

1/4 CUP PLAIN YOGURT

2 GARLIC CLOVES, CRUSHED

1 TABLESPOON OLIVE OIL

JUICE 1 LEMON

◆ Place chicken fillets in a shallow dish. In a bowl, mix together lemon juice, 2 tablespoons olive oil, salt, and pepper. Pour over chicken, cover, and refrigerate 1 hour.

◆ To make hummus, place chickpeas, tahini, yogurt, garlic, olive oil, lemon juice, salt, and pepper in a blender or food processor and process to form a slightly grainy paste.

◆ Put chicken fillets in the basket and place in the rotisserie. Cook 25 to 30 minutes at 425°F, until cooked through. Cut into slices and keep warm.

◆ Mix together sesame seeds, cumin, paprika, and salt. Drizzle bread on both sides with olive oil and toast under the grill.

◆ Spread some hummus on each piece of toast, top with chicken slices, and sprinkle with sesame seed mixture. Drizzle with remaining olive oil and serve, garnished with salad leaves.

Chicken Drumsticks with Spicy Fish Sauce

MAKES 4 TO 6 SERVINGS

1 OR 2 GARLIC CLOVES, CHOPPED

1 OR 2 STALKS LEMONGRASS, CHOPPED

2 SHALLOTS, CHOPPED

1 OR 2 SMALL RED OR GREEN CHILES, CHOPPED

1 TABLESPOON CHOPPED FRESH CILANTRO

1/4 CUP FISH SAUCE

6 TO 8 CHICKEN DRUMSTICKS, SKINNED

LETTUCE LEAVES, TO SERVE

SPICY FISH SAUCE

2 GARLIC CLOVES

2 SMALL RED OR GREEN CHILES, SEEDED-AND CHOPPED

1 TABLESPOON SUGAR

2 TABLESPOONS LIME JUICE

2 TABLESPOONS FISH SAUCE

◆ Using a mortar and pestle, pound garlic, lemongrass, shallots, chiles, and cilantro to a paste. In a mixing bowl, thoroughly blend pounded mixture with fish sauce to a smooth paste.

◆ Add drumsticks and coat well with the paste, then cover the bowl and let marinate in the refrigerator 2 to 3 hours, turning drumsticks every 30 minutes or so.

◆ To make spicy fish sauce, pound garlic and chiles until finely ground using a mortar and pestle. Transfer mixture to a bowl and add sugar, lime juice, fish sauce, and 2 or 3 tablespoons water. Blend well. Set aside.

◆ Put chicken drumsticks in the basket and place in the rotisserie. Cook 25 to 30 minutes at 425°F.

◆ Serve drumsticks hot on a bed of lettuce leaves with spicy fish sauce as a dip.

Chicken Wings with Coleslaw

MAKES 3 OR 4 SERVINGS

1/2 CUP SOY SAUCE

1/4 CUP TOMATO KETCHUP

1/4 CUP WHITE WINE VINEGAR

1/4 CUP CLEAR HONEY

1 GARLIC CLOVE, CRUSHED

1 TEASPOON GROUND GINGER

PINCH CHILI POWDER

8 CHICKEN WINGS

COLESLAW

1 CUP FINELY SHREDDED RED CABBAGE

1 CUP FINELY SHREDDED WHITE CABBAGE

1 CARROT, SHREDDED

1 TABLESPOON CHOPPED FRESH PARSLEY

2 TEASPOONS CHOPPED FRESH DILL

1/4 CUP OLIVE OIL

1 TABLESPOON SOY SAUCE

◆ Put soy sauce, tomato ketchup, vinegar, honey, garlic, ginger, and chili powder in an ovenproof dish and mix well. Add chicken wings and turn to coat thoroughly. Cover and refrigerate overnight.

◆ To make coleslaw, place red and white cabbage, carrot, parsley, dill, olive oil, and soy sauce in a bowl and mix together. Set aside.

◆ Put chicken wings in the basket and place in the rotisserie. Cook 30 to 35 minutes at 425°F. Serve with coleslaw.

Turkey Steaks Milanese

4 TURKEY FILLET STEAKS

1 TABLESPOON BUTTER

2 TABLESPOONS OLIVE OIL

4 GARLIC CLOVES, HALVED

2/3 CUP DRY WHITE WINE

1 1/4 CUPS WELL-FLAVORED
TURKEY OR CHICKEN STOCK

1 TEASPOON CORNSTARCH

1/3 CUP LIGHT CREAM

2 FRESH ROSEMARY SPRIGS OR
1 TEASPOON DRIED ROSEMARY

GREMOLATA

2 TABLESPOONS CHOPPED PARSLEY

GRATED ZEST 1 LEMON

1 GARLIC CLOVE, FINELY CHOPPED

◆ Brush turkey steaks with oil and put in the basket. Place in the rotisserie and cook 25 to 30 minutes at 425°F.

◆ Meanwhile, heat butter and remaining oil in a skillet and add garlic. Cook until pale golden, then pour off excess fat.

◆ Add wine and stock. Break sprig of rosemary into 2 or 3 pieces and add to pan. Cover and simmer 15 to 20 minutes.

◆ To make gremolata, in a small bowl, combine parsley, lemon, and chopped garlic. Set aside.

◆ Transfer turkey to a serving dish and keep warm. Remove garlic and rosemary from pan and discard.

◆ Blend cornstarch with cream and stir into sauce. Simmer to thicken and season to taste.

◆ To serve, pour sauce over turkey steaks and sprinkle with gremolata.

Turkey Burgers with Cranberry Relish

MAKES 4 SERVINGS

1¹/2 POUNDS GROUND TURKEY

1 SHALLOT, FINELY CHOPPED

2 TABLESPOONS CHOPPED FRESH THYME

2 TABLESPOONS GRATED ORANGE ZEST

SALT AND GROUND BLACK PEPPER

8 SLICES SOURDOUGH RYE BREAD

CORN SALAD

MAYONNAISE

CRANBERRY RELISH

¹/2 CUP CRANBERRY SAUCE

1 TABLESPOON GOLDEN RAISINS

1 TABLESPOON CHOPPED FRESH THYME

1 ORANGE, SEGMENTED AND
COARSELY CHOPPED

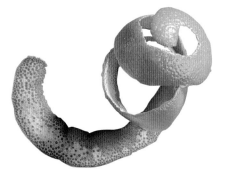

◆ Place turkey, shallot, thyme, orange zest and seasoning in a bowl and mix well to combine. Divide mixture into 4 portions and shape into patties.

◆ Brush burgers with a little oil. Put burgers in the bsket and place in the rotisserie. Cook 20-25 minutes at 425°F until cooked through. Meanwhile toast slices of bread lightly.

◆ To make cranberry relish, place cranberry sauce, golden raisins, thyme, and orange in a bowl and toss gently to combine. Chill until required.

◆ To serve, divide corn salad between 4 slices of bread, top with mayonnaise and a burger and place of spoonful of relish on each burger. Top burgers with remaining slices of bread and serve at once with extra cranberry relish and mayonnaise.

Vietnamese Roast Duck

MAKES 4 TO 6 SERVINGS

1 TEASPOON MINCED GARLIC

2 OR 3 SHALLOTS, FINELY CHOPPED

2 TEASPOONS FIVE-SPICE POWDER

2 TABLESPOONS SUGAR

1/4 CUP RED RICE VINEGAR

1 TABLESPOON FISH SAUCE

1 TABLESPOON SOY SAUCE

4 QUARTER DUCK PORTIONS
(2 BREASTS AND 2 LEGS)

1 CUP COCONUT MILK

SALT AND GROUND BLACK PEPPER

WATERCRESS, TO SERVE

CILANTRO SPRIGS, TO GARNISH

◆ In a large bowl, mix garlic, shallots, five-spice powder, sugar, vinegar, fish sauce, and soy sauce.

◆ Add duck and turn to coat evenly. Let marinate at least 2 to 3 hours, or overnight in the refrigerator, turning occasionally.

◆ Remove duck portions from marinade and put in the basket. Place in the rotisserie and cook 45 minutes at 425°F. Remove duck from rotisserie and keep warm.

◆ In a pan, heat marinade with juices that have collected in the drip tray. Add coconut milk, bring to boil, and simmer 5 minutes. Season with salt and pepper, then pour sauce into a serving bowl.

◆ Serve duck portions on a bed of watercress, garnished with cilantro sprigs.

Note: Duck portions can be chopped through the bone into bite-size pieces for serving, if wished.

Tunisian Lamb Burgers

1 POUND GROUND LAMB

1 SMALL ONION, FINELY CHOPPED

1 GARLIC CLOVE, CRUSHED

1/2 TEASPOON GROUND CUMIN

1/2 TEASPOON GROUND CORIANDER

1/2 OR 1 TEASPOON HARISSA PASTE

2 TEASPOONS CHOPPED FRESH OREGANO

2 TEASPOONS CHOPPED FRESH PARSLEY

OLIVE OIL FOR BRUSHING

TOMATO SALSA

2 LARGE TOMATOES, PEELED AND SEEDED

1/4 CUCUMBER, PEELED, QUARTERED, AND SEEDED

1 SMALL RED ONION

1 GARLIC CLOVE, CRUSHED

SALT AND GROUND BLACK PEPPER

GRATED ZEST 1/2 LEMON

◆ To make tomato salsa, roughly chop tomatoes, cucumber, and onion. Put in a food processor or blender with garlic and process until finely chopped.

◆ Season salsa with salt and pepper and stir in lemon zest. Transfer to a serving bowl, cover, and refrigerate until required.

◆ In a large bowl, mix together lamb, onion, garlic, cumin, coriander, harissa paste, oregano, parsley, and salt until well combined. Form into 4 burgers and brush lightly with oil.

◆ Put burgers in the basket and place in the rotisserie. Cook 15 to 20 minutes at 425°F. Serve with tomato salsa.

Mediterranean Lamb Chops

MAKES 4 SERVINGS

8 SMALL BONELESS LAMB LOIN CHOPS

6 GARLIC CLOVES, CRUSHED

2 TABLESPOONS TOMATO PASTE

1/4 CUP OLIVE OIL

2 TABLESPOONS RED WINE VINEGAR

2 TEASPOONS PAPRIKA

2 TABLESPOONS CHOPPED FRESH
ROSEMARY OR MINT

2 TEASPOONS CORIANDER SEEDS,
CRUSHED

FRESH HERBS, TO GARNISH

GREEN SALAD, TO SERVE (OPTIONAL)

◆ Place lamb chops in a shallow glass dish. In a small bowl, mix together garlic, tomato paste, olive oil, red wine vinegar, paprika, chopped rosemary or mint and crushed coriander seeds.

◆ Spread marinade over chops, turn them over, and coat with rest of mixture. Cover and refrigerate at least 2 hours or overnight.

◆ Bring chops to room temperature before cooking. Put in the basket and place in the rotisserie. Cook 20 to 25 minutes at 425°F.

◆ Serve with green salad, if desired.

Note: Use boneless chops or leg steaks if preferred.

Teriyaki Ribs

MAKES 2 OR 3 SERVINGS

1/4 CUP CLEAR HONEY

2 TABLESPOONS DARK SOY SAUCE

1/4 CUP TOMATO KETCHUP

1 TEASPOON CRACKED BLACK PEPPER

1 1/2 TEASPOONS CHINESE FIVE-SPICE POWDER

GRATED ZEST AND JUICE 1 SMALL ORANGE

1 1/2 POUNDS MEATY PORK SPARERIBS

SALAD AND CRUSTY BREAD, TO SERVE
(OPTIONAL)

◆ In a bowl, mix together honey, soy sauce, tomato ketchup, black pepper, Chinese five-spice powder, and orange zest and juice.

◆ Place spareribs in a large glass dish and pour marinade over them. Turn ribs to coat evenly. Cover and refrigerate 2 to 3 hours, if time permits.

◆ Remove ribs from marinade, put in the basket, and place in the rotisserie. Cook 30 to 40 minutes at 425°F.

◆ Serve hot ribs with salad and crusty bread, if desired.

Spareribs with Tangy Barbecue Sauce

MAKES 2 OR 3 SERVINGS

1 GARLIC CLOVE, CRUSHED

1/4 CUP CLEAR HONEY

1 TABLESPOON TOMATO PASTE

1 TABLESPOON CHILI SAUCE

1 TABLESPOON WORCESTERSHIRE SAUCE

1 TABLESPOON SOY SAUCE

2 TEASPOONS AMERICAN YELLOW MUSTARD

JUICE 1 LEMON

1 1/2 POUNDS MEATY PORK SPARERIBS

◆ In a bowl, mix together garlic, honey, tomato paste, chili sauce, Worcestershire sauce, soy sauce, mustard, and lemon juice.

◆ Place spareribs in a large glass dish and pour sauce over ribs, turning ribs to coat evenly. Cover and refrigerate 2 hours, if time permits.

◆ Remove ribs from barbecue sauce and pour remaining sauce into a small saucepan.

◆ Put ribs in the basket and place in the rotisserie. Cook 30 to 40 minutes at 425°F.

◆ Just before serving, reheat sauce. Bring sauce to a boil and boil rapidly 2 or 3 minutes.

◆ Serve ribs hot, passing sauce separately.

Stuffed Fillet of Pork with Apple Sauce

2 PORK FILLETS, EACH WEIGHING
1 POUND

1 LEMON, THINLY SLICED

16 GARLIC CLOVES, PEELED

16 FRESH BAY LEAVES

3 TABLESPOONS OLIVE OIL

1 TABLESPOON BUTTER

3 GREEN DESSERT APPLES

1 TABLESPOON BROWN SUGAR

1 TABLESPOON BALSAMIC VINEGAR

PARSLEY PESTO

1/2 GARLIC CLOVE, CHOPPED

1/4 TEASPOON SEA SALT

1/3 CUP CHOPPED FRESH PARSLEY

2 TABLESPOONS PINE NUTS, TOASTED

1/2 TEASPOON GRATED LEMON ZEST

1 1/2 TABLESPOONS CAPERS

1/4 CUP OLIVE OIL

1 TABLESPOON FRESHLY GRATED
PARMESAN CHEESE

GROUND BLACK PEPPER

◆ To make parsley pesto, blend garlic, salt, parsley, pine nuts, lemon zest, and capers in a blender or food processor until fairly smooth. Transfer to a bowl. Stir in olive oil, Parmesan, and pepper until combined and season to taste.

◆ Wash and dry pork. Use a sharp knife to cut along length of each fillet, without cutting in half. Open out fillets and cover with pesto.

◆ Cut lemon slices in half and arrange in center of pork with garlic cloves. Tie each stuffed fillet back together with string at 1-inch intervals. Tuck bay leaves under string along length of fillets. Cover and place in refrigerator to marinate overnight.

◆ Put fillets in the basket and place in the rotisserie. Cook 40 to 50 minutes at 425°F.

◆ Meanwhile, heat remaining oil in a pan with butter. Quarter, core, and thickly slice apples and fry 2 or 3 minutes on each side until golden. Remove with a slotted spoon. Stir sugar and vinegar into pan. Add to apples and set aside.

◆ Remove pork, cover with aluminum foil and let stand 5 minutes while finishing sauce. Pour all pork juices from the drip tray into a pan and add apples and juice. Bring to a boil, then simmer 2 or 3 minutes until thick.

◆ Cut pork into thick slices and serve with apple sauce.

Note: Parsley pesto can be made in double this quantity and stored in a clean jar in the refrigerator up to 5 days.

Pork with Herb Sauce

MAKES 4 SERVINGS

1/2 CUP FRESH WHITE BREADCRUMBS

2 TABLESPOONS WHITE WINE VINEGAR

2 GARLIC CLOVES

2 CANNED ANCHOVY FILLETS, DRAINED

1/4 CUP CHOPPED FRESH PARSLEY

2 TEASPOONS CAPERS

1 HARD-BOILED EGG YOLK

1 CUP EXTRA VIRGIN OLIVE OIL

SALT AND GROUND BLACK PEPPER

4 PORK LOIN CHOPS, ABOUT 1 INCH THICK

◆ In a small bowl, soak breadcrumbs in white wine vinegar.

◆ Meanwhile, using a mortar and pestle, crush garlic with anchovy fillets, parsley, capers, and egg yolk. Transfer to a bowl.

◆ Squeeze vinegar from breadcrumbs, then mix breadcrumbs into mixture in bowl. Stir in oil in a slow trickle to make a creamy sauce. Add black pepper, and salt if necessary. Set aside.

◆ Put chops in the basket and place in the rotisserie. Cook 25 to 30 minutes at 425°F, until cooked through but still juicy in the center.

◆ Transfer chops to 4 warmed serving plates and season with salt and pepper. Spoon on some sauce and serve remaining sauce separately.

Jerk Pork

1 TABLESPOON OIL

2 ONIONS, FINELY CHOPPED

2 FRESH RED CHILES, SEEDED AND
FINELY CHOPPED

1 GARLIC CLOVE, CRUSHED

1-INCH PIECE FRESH GINGER, GRATED

1 TEASPOON DRIED THYME

1 TEASPOON GROUND ALLSPICE

1 TEASPOON GROUND CINNAMON

1 TEASPOON HOT PEPPER SAUCE

JUICE 1 LARGE ORANGE

GRATED ZEST AND JUICE 1 LIME

2 TEASPOONS BROWN SUGAR

SALT AND GROUND BLACK PEPPER

4 PORK STEAKS OR CHOPS

◆ In a skillet, heat oil. Add onions and cook 10 minutes until soft.

◆ Add chiles, garlic, ginger, thyme, allspice, and cinnamon and fry 2 minutes.

◆ Stir in hot pepper sauce, orange juice, lime zest and juice, and sugar. Simmer until mixture forms a dark paste. Season and let cool.

◆ Place pork steaks or chops in a shallow dish and rub paste over. Cover and refrigerate overnight.

◆ Put steaks or chops in the basket and place in the rotisserie. Cook 25 to 30 minutes at 425°F.

Chili Burger

MAKES 4 SERVINGS

2 TABLESPOONS VEGETABLE OIL

1 ONION, FINELY CHOPPED

2 GARLIC CLOVES, CRUSHED

1 TABLESPOON CRUSHED CHILI FLAKES

2 TEASPOONS GROUND CUMIN

1 1/2 POUNDS GROUND BEEF

2 TABLESPOONS SUN-DRIED TOMATO PASTE

1/4 CUP CHOPPED FRESH CILANTRO

4 WHEAT TORTILLAS, WARMED THROUGH

COS LETTUCE LEAVES, ONION RINGS, AND SLICED TOMATO, TO SERVE

◆ Heat oil in a pan and cook onion and garlic 3 minutes until soft. Add crushed chili flakes and cumin and cook an additional 2 minutes. Set aside to cool.

◆ Place beef in a bowl. Add cooked onion mixture, sun-dried tomato paste, cilantro, and seasoning, and mix well to combine.

◆ Divide mixture into 4 equal portions and shape into patties.

◆ Put burgers in the basket and place in the rotisserie. Cook 15 to 20 minutes at 425°F.

◆ Serve each burger in a warm tortilla with lettuce, onion, and tomato.

Hickory Burgers

MAKES 4 SERVINGS

1 1/2 POUNDS GROUND SIRLOIN STEAK

1 SMALL ONION, FINELY CHOPPED

1/4 CUP BARBECUE SAUCE

2 TABLESPOONS CHOPPED FRESH PARSLEY

SALT AND GROUND BLACK PEPPER

BUTTER, SOFTENED

4 HAMBURGER BUNS, SPLIT LENGTHWISE

LETTUCE LEAVES, TOMATO AND SLICED GREEN PEPPERS, TO GARNISH

SLICED DILL PICKLES AND EXTRA BARBECUE SAUCE, TO SERVE

◆ Place beef, onion, barbecue sauce, parsley and seasoning in a bowl and mix well to combine.

◆ Divide mixture into 4 equal portions and shape into patties.

◆ Put burgers in the basket and place in the rotisserie. Cook at 425°F 15 to 20 minutes.

◆ Butter cut sides of buns sparingly and toast lightly.

◆ To serve, divide salad garnish between 4 bottom halves of buns. Place a burger on each, top with dill pickles and then with bun tops. Serve with extra barbecue sauce passed separately.

Fruity Sausage Balls

MAKES 20

1 POUND GOOD-QUALITY,
WELL-FLAVORED SAUSAGES

1^1/2 CUPS PITTED PRUNES

1 CUP HAZELNUTS, CHOPPED

1^1/4 CUPS STOCK

1/3 CUP REDCURRANT JELLY

LEMON JUICE, TO TASTE

SALT AND GROUND BLACK PEPPER

◆ Slit sausage skins and remove meat. Chop half the prunes and mix with sausage meat and hazelnuts. Form into 20 small balls.

◆ Put in the basket and place in the rotisserie. Cook 20 to 25 minutes at 425°F.

◆ In a blender, purée remaining prunes with chicken stock and redcurrant jelly. Add lemon juice, salt, and pepper to taste.

◆ Pour sauce into a small saucepan and bring just to a boil. Transfer to a warm serving bowl.

◆ To serve, put fruity sausage balls on a warm serving plate and a stand dish of sauce in the center.

Dips and Sauces

Tomato Sauce

MAKES 4 TO 6 SERVINGS

2 TABLESPOONS OLIVE OIL

1/2 SPANISH ONION

1/2 GARLIC CLOVE, CHOPPED

1 RED BELL PEPPER, CHOPPED

2 POUNDS BEEFSTEAK TOMATOES,
PEELED, SEEDED, AND CHOPPED

SUGAR AND/OR TOMATO PASTE (OPTIONAL)

SALT AND GROUND BLACK PEPPER

◆ Heat oil in a skillet, add onion, and cook slowly 5 minutes.

◆ Stir in garlic and red bell pepper and continue to cook slowly an additional 10 minutes, stirring occasionally.

◆ Stir tomatoes into pan. Simmer gently 20 to 30 minutes, stirring occasionally, until thickened.

◆ Add sugar and/or tomato paste, if desired, and season with salt and pepper.

◆ Put sauce into a blender or food processor, or pass through a fine non-metallic strainer, if desired.

Barbecue Sauce

MAKES 4 TO 6 SERVINGS

2 GARLIC CLOVES, CRUSHED

8-OUNCE CAN PINEAPPLE IN FRUIT JUICE,
DRAINED AND ROUGHLY CHOPPED

8-OUNCE CAN CHOPPED TOMATOES

3 TABLESPOONS CIDER VINEGAR

2 TABLESPOONS SOFT BROWN SUGAR

2 TABLESPOONS MANGO CHUTNEY

2 TEASPOONS WORCESTERSHIRE SAUCE

1/2 TEASPOON SMOOTH MUSTARD

1/2 TEASPOON MIXED SPICE

FEW DROPS TABASCO SAUCE

SALT AND PEPPER

1 TABLESPOON CORNSTARCH

◆ Put garlic, pineapple, tomatoes, vinegar, sugar, mango chutney, Worcestershire sauce, mustard, mixed spice, Tabasco sauce, and salt and pepper in a saucepan and stir well.

◆ Bring slowly to boil, cover and simmer gently 10 minutes, stirring occasionally. Remove pan from heat and set aside to cool.

◆ Once cool, purée sauce in a blender or food processor until smooth. Return sauce to saucepan.

◆ In a small bowl, blend cornstarch with 1 tablespoon water. Stir cornstarch mixture into sauce and bring slowly to a boil, stirring continuously.

◆ Simmer sauce gently 3 minutes and adjust seasoning to taste before serving.

Broiled Tomato and Chili Sauce

MAKES 4 SERVINGS

2 POUNDS PLUM TOMATOES

4 LARGE GARLIC CLOVES, UNPEELED

2 FRESH GREEN CHILES

2 TEASPOONS DRIED OREGANO OR THYME

2 TABLESPOONS OLIVE OIL

1/2 ONION, FINELY CHOPPED

1/2 TEASPOON SUGAR

1/2 TEASPOON SALT

GROUND BLACK PEPPER

1 TABLESPOON BUTTER

◆ Broil tomatoes, garlic, and chiles, turning frequently, until skins blister and blacken.

◆ Peel garlic, remove skin and seeds from chile, but do not peel tomatoes.

◆ Dry-fry oregano in a small heavy-bottomed pan a few minutes until you can smell the aroma.

◆ Heat oil in another small pan. Gently fry onion about 5 minutes until translucent. Add oregano and fry 1 minute.

◆ Purée tomatoes, including any blackened bits of skin (they add to the flavor), with garlic, chile, and onion mixture until smooth.

◆ Pour into a large skillet and season with sugar, salt, and black pepper. Simmer 5 to 10 minutes, stirring occasionally, until some of the liquid has evaporated. Stir in butter.

Warm Salsa Verde

MAKES 6 TO 8 SERVINGS

2 OR 3 JALAPEÑO CHILES

6 TO 8 GREEN ONIONS

1 OR 2 GARLIC CLOVES, CRUSHED

1/2 CUP CAPERS, RINSED

1 BUNCH FRESH PARSLEY

1/2 BUNCH FRESH TARRAGON, DILL, CILANTRO, OR MINT

1 CUP EXTRA VIRGIN OLIVE OIL

GRATED ZEST AND JUICE 1 LARGE LEMON

STRIPS LEMON PEEL, TO GARNISH

◆ Seed and coarsely chop chiles. Coarsely chop green onions.

◆ Put chiles, green onions, and garlic into a food processor fitted with a metal blade, and process until blended, scraping down side of the bowl once or twice.

◆ Add capers and herbs and, using pulse button, process until finely chopped.

◆ In a medium saucepan over low heat, heat olive oil until warm. Stir in herb mixture and immediately remove pan from heat.

◆ Add lemon zest and juice and season with a little salt.

◆ Serve warm, garnished with strips of lemon peel.

Spicy Hamburger Relish

MAKES 12 TO 14 SERVINGS

3 TABLESPOONS OLIVE OIL

1 ONION, FINELY CHOPPED

1 RED BELL PEPPER, CHOPPED

2 OR 3 GARLIC CLOVES, FINELY CHOPPED

1-INCH PIECE FRESH GINGER,
FINELY CHOPPED

6 LARGE RIPE TOMATOES, PEELED AND
CUT INTO 1/2-INCH PIECES

1 TEASPOON DRIED CHILI FLAKES

1 TEASPOON GROUND CINNAMON

1 TEASPOON GROUND NUTMEG

SALT AND GROUND BLACK PEPPER

1/3 CUP BALSAMIC OR CIDER VINEGAR

3/4 CUP LIGHT OR DARK BROWN SUGAR

1 OR 2 TABLESPOONS CHOPPED CILANTRO

◆ In a medium, heavy-bottomed saucepan over medium heat, heat olive oil. Add onion, red bell pepper, garlic, and fresh ginger and cook 5 or 6 minutes until beginning to soften, stirring frequently.

◆ Add tomatoes, cover, and cook gently about 5 minutes, stirring occasionally.

◆ Stir in chili flakes, cinnamon, nutmeg, salt and pepper, vinegar, and sugar and bring to a boil, stirring to dissolve sugar.

◆ Simmer about 20 minutes until liquid has evaporated and vegetables are tender.

◆ Remove from heat and stir in cilantro. Let cool.

Note: Stored in the refrigerator in a glass or plastic container with an airtight cover, this sauce will keep up to 1 week.

Variation: Substitute fresh parsley for cilantro.

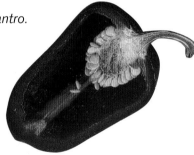

Mayonnaise

MAKES 6 SERVINGS

2 EGG YOLKS

1 TEASPOON DIJON-STYLE MUSTARD

1 TABLESPOON LEMON JUICE OR
WHITE WINE VINEGAR

PINCH CASTER SUGAR

GROUND BLACK PEPPER AND
1/2 TEASPOON SALT

1 1/4 CUPS LIGHT OLIVE OIL

◆ Put eggs yolks, mustard, lemon juice or vinegar, sugar, salt, and black pepper to taste in a small blender or food processor and blend about 20 seconds, until smooth, pale, and creamy.

◆ With motor running, gradually pour in oil in a slow, steady stream until mayonnaise is thick, creamy and smooth. Adjust seasoning.

Lemon Mayonnaise Use lemon juice and stir in 1 1/2 teaspoons finely grated lemon zest before serving.

Garlic and Herb Mayonnaise Add 1 crushed garlic clove with egg yolks and stir in 2 tablespoons chopped fresh herbs before serving.

Broiled Corn Salsa

MAKES 10 TO 12 SERVINGS

2 LARGE EARS CORN

1 RED OR LARGE SWEET ONION,
FINELY CHOPPED

4 RIPE PLUM TOMATOES,
SEEDED AND COARSELY CHOPPED

1 GARLIC CLOVE, FINELY CHOPPED

2 JALAPEÑO CHILES,
SEEDED AND FINELY CHOPPED

1 BUNCH CILANTRO,
TRIMMED AND FINELY CHOPPED

SALT AND GROUND BLACK PEPPER

◆ Cook corn in plenty of boiling water about 15 minutes until tender. Drain.

◆ Broil corn, or grill over hot coals, turning occasionally, about 10 minutes. Let cool.

◆ Hold corn vertically at a slight angle to the chopping board, stem end down. Using a sharp knife, cut down along cob to remove kernels. Place kernels in a large bowl and repeat with remaining corn.

◆ Using a sharp knife, scrape along each cob, removing remaining "milk" and add this to the bowl. Stir in onion.

◆ Add tomatoes, garlic, chiles, cilantro, salt, and black pepper. Toss together and spoon into a serving bowl.

◆ Let stand about 30 minutes before serving.

Olive and Cilantro Relish

MAKES 4 SERVINGS

2 RED BELL PEPPERS

1 1/2 CUPS BLACK OLIVES IN OIL,
PITTED AND FINELY SLICED

1/2 FRESH GREEN CHILE, SEEDED AND
VERY FINELY CHOPPED

1/3 CUP FINELY CHOPPED CILANTRO LEAVES

1 TABLESPOON LEMON JUICE

GROUND BLACK PEPPER

1/3 CUP OLIVE OIL

LETTUCE LEAVES AND 1 HARD-BOILED EGG,
QUARTERED, TO SERVE

◆ Broil bell peppers about 10 minutes, turning occasionally, until skins begin to blacken. Cover or place in a sealed plastic bag 5 minutes.

◆ Remove skin and seeds and cut flesh into small dice. Mix with olives, chile, and cilantro in a bowl.

◆ Whisk together lemon juice, black pepper, and olive oil and pour over olive mixture. Let stand at room temperature 1 hour.

◆ Pile mixture on a bed of lettuce leaves and top with hard-boiled egg quarters to serve.

Index